God
has daughters too

Text copyright © Abidemi Sanusi 2006
The author asserts the moral right
to be identified as the author of this work

Published by
The Bible Reading Fellowship
First Floor, Elsfield Hall
15–17 Elsfield Way, Oxford OX2 8FG
Website: www.brf.org.uk

ISBN-10: 1 84101 417 6
ISBN-13: 978 1 84101 417 3

First published 2006
10 9 8 7 6 5 4 3 2 1 0
All rights reserved

Acknowledgments

Unless otherwise stated, scripture quotations are taken from the Holy Bible, New
International Version, copyright © 1973, 1978, 1984 by International Bible Society, and
are used by permission of Hodder & Stoughton Limited. All rights reserved. 'NIV' is a
registered trademark of International Bible Society. UK trademark number 1448790.

Scripture quotations taken from the New Revised Standard Version of the Bible,
Anglicized Edition, copyright © 1989, 1995 by the Division of Christian Education of the
National Council of the Churches of Christ in the USA are used by permission. All rights
reserved.

Scripture quotations taken from the Contemporary English Version of the Bible published
by HarperCollins Publishers, copyright © 1991, 1992, 1995 American Bible Society.

Scripture quotations taken from the New American Standard Bible, ©1960, 1962, 1963,
1968, 1971, 1972, 1973, 1975, 1977, 1995 by The Lockman Foundation. Used by
permission.

Scripture quotations marked NLT are taken from the Holy Bible, New Living Translation,
© 1996. Used by permission of Tyndale House Publishers, Inc., Wheaton, Illinois 60189.
All rights reserved.

A catalogue record for this book is available from the British Library

Printed in Singapore by Craft Print International Ltd

God
has daughters too

ABIDEMI SANUSI

For the Holy Spirit, who continues to remind me that without him, I truly cannot write. And for every woman who has yet to find the Way.

A big thank you to God's daughters: my mother, Gloria Ademokun, and Amanda Dye

Contents

Introduction

I am a fiction writer and avid fiction reader. I love the way scriptural truths can be woven into stories that leap out of the page at readers. I believe that people respond to fiction because of its dramatic value. It is this dramatic value that I sought to achieve in writing this book. I wanted to take readers down the road of biblical history as witnessed by the women profiled.

I've often wondered about the Bible. Why do people believe that it is no longer relevant, that the events narrated within are either of no consequence or, even worse, didn't happen at all, despite overwhelming evidence to the contrary? I believe one of the primary reasons the Lord gave us the Bible was so that we would identify with the people and the events in the book, to equip us to deal with our challenges rather than feeling alienated or overwhelmed by them.

Although the women profiled in this book lived in exceptional times, the issues, choices and lives they experienced are, in many ways, not so very different from what we face today. These are women who endured trying circumstances and who allowed God to demonstrate his grace in their lives, even if, outwardly, things did not necessarily improve.

I have selected these particular women because of the challenges or issues that defined their character, faith or both. Leah was a 'married single', Gomer was promiscuous, Deborah was a judge, while Esther was a beauty queen who prevented her people's genocide. Michal had some choices taken from her, while Gomer made decisions herself, only to realize that what she thought she wanted wasn't what she needed. I want to show how God worked in each woman's situation to accomplish his will, sometimes despite, as much as because of, the character concerned.

You will notice that this book promotes the idea that everyone who dies is fully aware of events taking place on earth. I lifted this theology—mine, I should add—from Hebrews 12:1, which makes reference to the departed saints and angelic hosts looking down on us and cheering us on in our Christian faith. I've taken that literally to mean that they have an overview on other events in the Bible as well as on earth today. And for the women profiled whose afterlife destination is unknown, I have taken creative licence and hinted at where they might be, because I certainly don't know for sure! At times—not too often, I hope—I have taken dramatic liberties for purely creative reasons.

Some readers may be somewhat discomfited by the idea that a few of the women profiled appear to be rather negative, even though they are in heaven. I have taken the line that being present with the Lord does not mean losing the unique personality traits with which he endowed each individual while on earth—and that these characters are continuing to work through their issues in heaven!

Eve: broken families and a murderer for a son

I wasn't always known as 'The one who gave Adam the fruit', 'The sin bringer', 'Mother of Cain the first murderer'. I had a name—Eve, which means 'living'. My other titles are 'The first woman' and 'Mother of humanity', but most people prefer to call me by 'The one who brought about the Fall'. I don't mind. I'm quite used to it. After all, what are titles? However, I do get really annoyed when people conveniently forget that Adam was with me the whole time that the Fall debacle was taking place. He could easily have decided not to partake of the fruit with me. God gave him a will. It's not my fault he didn't use it when I was talking to that serpent. But I digress.

I look out from heaven and I can see how alike women are. I can see your prayers shooting up like lights. All day and all night, you beseech the king with your prayers: 'Have mercy on my son. He's yours, Lord. Protect him and guide him. He's just a bit confused but I know he'll come round.' I know the feeling. I've been there. I carried Cain for nine months; he nursed at my breasts, as did his brother, Abel. They roamed, played and grew up in what you would call modern-day Iraq. They were brothers, and my children. Then Cain, my own son, killed Abel, my other son. I should have seen it coming, but I didn't. Sure, they were different and always at each other's throats, but they were boys—and boys are boisterous. Ask anyone with boys and they'll tell you just how boisterous they are. But I never thought one of them would end up killing the other. So not only did I get Adam and myself sent out of Eden, I spawned a murderer.

I am also internationally and spiritually known as 'The sin bringer'. In fact, if I didn't know any better, I would think my life was a disaster from day one. If God knew that the Fall would occur, why did he bother giving Adam and me free will? He certainly would have saved himself the grief of sin and its effects on humans. After the Fall, I asked him that question again and again, and all he would say was that he couldn't have a relationship with robots who were unable to exercise their independent will. With humans, both parties had a choice regarding whether or not to accept the relationship offered. His explanation sometimes made me feel better, sometimes a lot worse, as I didn't think I deserved to be loved by God—because of my part in the Fall. I guess that's humans for you—never satisfied with what they have, even if it is God's unconditional love.

Hard times

I am not really sure how I coped on earth during those trying times after Cain murdered my son, but I do know how God coped with me. It seemed that my dreams of family perfection had turned into ashes. There were times when I really hated Cain, hated him with every fibre of my being, and there were times when I loved him so much—even when God put that mark on him, after he killed his brother, to protect him from harm. Sometimes I think God did that to protect him from me. There were times when I would wake up with the sole intention of killing him, because my pain at losing Abel was so great.

Sometimes I blamed God. He knew that Cain had an inferiority complex when it came to Abel. Why couldn't he just have accepted Cain's vegetable and plant offering? Cain was a farmer and he thought he was giving God the best of his toil. Abel was a shepherd and he gave God his choicest flock. They were both giving the best of what they had, weren't they? So why did God refuse Cain's gift and make him so angry that he killed his own brother out of sheer jealousy? It was all God's fault, I would reason to myself. He sees the end from the beginning. He knew that Abel would die, yet he did absolutely nothing about it.

Other times, I would go to Abel's grave and just weep, overwhelmed by sorrow. Who knows and understands the grief of a mother except God himself? And let me tell you, when Jesus was nailed to the cross, I saw the Father look away as his Son became sin personified. I saw his grief and was once again reminded of that day in the garden when the serpent enticed me with promises of divine knowledge. I cannot wait for the day when he will be cast into the pit of fire for ever. Fiend. But I digress again.

Where was I? Yes, God and grief. Yes, he understands grief because he has experienced it himself, and don't let anyone tell you any different. During those dark days, I even wondered if I had made Cain kill his brother. After all, I caused the Fall (yes, we're back to that again) and brought sin into the world, didn't I? I would look at Adam and wonder what he was thinking. I mean, our family wouldn't feature on an advertisement for Jesus Family Inc. You know what I mean—serene smiles and halos as big as archangel Gabriel's wings. One night, Adam had the gall to say, 'Abel's death was not your fault.' I couldn't believe it. I think he thought he was comforting me, but he just made me so angry. The best thing he could have done for me then was to shut his mouth. But no, he was, as usual, trying to fix things. Well, on that occasion, he failed—miserably.

'I'm not blaming myself,' I told him. 'But it seems as if you might be blaming me. If I was a good mother, Cain would not have killed Abel. I should have known. I'm a mother; we know and see everything, don't we? No doubt, you'll be reporting to the Lord and telling him how inadequately suited I am to be your helpmate.' I lay awake that night, convinced that God would send an angel to distribute my remains outside Eden as a reminder of my failure as a mother and a wife. Yet, all of a sudden, a sweet fragrance permeated the forest area where we were bedding for the night. It was followed by a stillness and a peace that I knew could only come from the

Lord. His presence sustained me that night, as it still continues to sustain people everywhere today.

Looking back

I've had a lot of time to reflect since then. Of course, being in heaven, I have an overview of situations but, just so that you know, every family in the Bible and living on the earth today experiences challenges and strife. Yes, even the ones you see in church with the toothpaste-advert smiles. You don't believe me? Abraham, Isaac, Jacob, Samuel, David, Solomon and even Jesus himself experienced conflict. It couldn't have been easy for Jesus' brothers, having someone in the family saying deluded things like, 'I and the Father are one' (John 10:30). And there's all that stuff about their mother, Mary, being impregnated by the Holy Spirit. What distinguishes each family, though, is how they handled their interpersonal challenges. Some of them took matters into their hands and ended up in even finer messes. Others resolved to trust God even when it seemed obvious to everyone that God had a temporary case of amnesia when it came to their situation. It is these same people who are honoured in Hebrews 11, the Bible's 'hall of faith' chapter. It just goes to show that God *never* forgets.

I remember the first time I gave birth. Adam, bless him, hovered anxiously around me. The situation was comical, to say the least. We didn't know what to expect so we just did what came naturally. Well, you feel like pushing, so you push, and out comes a baby. The umbilical cord? Well, I wasn't going to have the infant hanging around me like some kind of albatross, so it had to go. 'Go ahead and cut it!' I yelled to Adam, who had a lost look on his face. And so it was with us as a family. We tried to train our children in the way they should go. We didn't always succeed but we gave it a shot.

And so should you. Life on earth means living in a fallen world— a world full of evil and incomprehensible violence. On the whole, we try to shield our families from evil influences but we cannot do that indefinitely. God in his infinite wisdom does not hide us from life's challenges, because he knows that we can learn something about ourselves and about him from those experiences. Shouldn't you, as a parent, do the same for your children? Of course no mother wants to bury her offspring. I buried my son, and I had to look into the eyes of his murderer—my other son. What pain, what anguish, and what evil! But was God's pain any less than mine when I partook of the forbidden fruit and ushered in a reign of sin? He could have shielded himself from that pain by creating robots instead of humans with independent will, but he chose not to do that. He didn't shield himself.

I remember going to Adam after Cain left for the country of Nod (which means 'wandering') and saying, 'My family is broken, never to be fixed. Life will never be the same again.' I was right. Things never were the same again. I had to learn how to rely on God even though I was plagued with guilt. Yes, guilt, every woman's burden. But one day, after Cain killed Abel, I went to Nod to see him. I looked at the mark on him and knew that I would do everything to help this boy—my son, the murderer. And I also knew that somehow God would take care of everything. I didn't know how things would turn out, but I knew that my family was in his hands and that all I needed to do was trust and pray. And here in heaven, I'm still trusting and praying for all God's children.

What is a model family?

We didn't have television in my day, so Adam and I didn't have any family 'role models' for comparison. We had the Trinity—Father, Son and Holy Spirit—which is always a better deal. In Eden, Adam and I saw how they flowed together, rather like a musical composition. The best way to describe this would be to use earth-speak: God says, 'Turn the light on', Jesus flicks the switch, and the Holy Spirit provides the electric current. I hope that explains it better. When we were banished, though, we found a rather unusual role model for our family: animals.

Ever watched an animal family? They're not so different from humans—honestly. When Adam had one of his 'I'm-not-a-man-I'm-a-little-boy' days, he simply went to watch the lions. He would come back from these trips with his strength restored a thousandfold. He used to tell me it was the lions' majesty that inspired him. I would tell him that it should inspire him to help me some more with the children and our daily business of living. Then he would feign ignorance of what I said and I'd give him the silent treatment for the rest of the day. The trouble is, we had no neighbours except the angel that guarded Eden, so I couldn't go and mouth off to anyone. Come night-time, Adam would reach out for me and I would crawl into his arms rather peevishly. I never could keep up a quarrel for long.

I've noticed that, on earth, a lot of women carry their marital hurts over to the next day. There's no sense in doing that. Do it for a week, a month, a year, and it builds up—and before long your mind is a cesspit of hurt and pain. The key is to live each day as the last, one day at a time. When Adam ate the fruit I gave him, I saw him in a different light, and, to be truthful, I wasn't sure that I liked what I saw. Just for a minute, I thought he was weak, and that made me uncomfortable. But God really helped us out. He made us clothes (pure leather, I'll have you know) and actually clothed us himself, much like Jesus covering those who believe in him with his own purity.

The first few days outside Eden were hard. It seemed as if, everywhere I looked, I saw accusing eyes. I would go past the angel guarding Eden and just keep my gaze fixed on the ground. I didn't want to see the disappointment on his face, the kind of disappointment I thought I saw in Adam's eyes every time he looked at me. Then, one day, my husband took me by the hand and said, 'This is our life now, and we'll make it work. God will see us through. I still blame you for taking the fruit from that serpent but, then again, no one forced me to eat it. I chose it freely.'

I bristled inwardly when he said he blamed me for what I'd done, but I let it pass. I had to—what else could I do? I was hungry and had no idea how to find food, much less cook it. I started thinking about Eden and how we were never hungry. We just ate plants and fruits whenever we felt like it, and everything was replenished by the Lord, much as things are in heaven. But anyway, there we were, Adam and I, and he'd just told me we had to move on. No point looking at the past. Adam wasn't to know it, but he had given me the basic strategy for surviving life in a fallen world. Eden was gone, lost for ever, and we had to look to the future. This meant facing life together, as one unit. It also meant leaving the 'blame game' at the gate of Eden—or as near to the gate as the angel would allow us to go. Instead of attacking each other, we had to attack the situation confronting us before it destroyed us completely as a couple and as a family. It was a strategy I wished I didn't have to employ when Abel was murdered. It would have been much easier to attack Adam, the Lord and everything else around me in my grief. I thought I was the only one suffering. After all, I was the woman, the life bearer, a title that I felt gave me the supreme right to emotional pain, to the point of being almost selfish about it. You may know what I mean because you may have done the same yourself. You may be in the midst of it as you're reading this and, like me, you probably think you earned the right to be selfish. You're the life bearer, for goodness' sake!

In my bereavement, I forgot that my family was hurting too. I might have lost a son, but so had my husband, and the rest of the family had lost a brother—or two, as Cain was banished. And that is how a tragedy such as ours can tear families apart. In our grief, we almost isolated each other. I thank God for granting Adam wisdom. He allowed me to grieve privately and gave me the confidence to reach out to my family so that we could grieve together. It was a painful time in our history, but in the end it drew us closer.

Strategies for survival

You may think that yours is the only family in church, or even on your street, presenting a distinctly inferior version of a godly family.

But the Lord's family is not inferior; he does not make mistakes. I wish I could give you a glimpse of my perspective and show you what God's family really looks like. On earth, they probably wouldn't have got a look in on your local Christian TV channel, but they pleased God in humanly inexplicable ways. Do you know why? They never forgot whose they were: they were God's children and a part of God's family.

Can I tell you who I'm sitting next to? I'm sitting next to a man who, while on earth, had to kill his own wife in a civil war because they were from different ethnic groups. It was either the wife or the children. He went on the rampage after that, killing people left and right until God gave him a revelation of heaven. He came to his senses and went back to his community to put his family together.

To my left is a young girl—I believe her earthly age was 16—who almost destroyed her family with her promiscuity, drugs and violence towards her siblings and mother. Actually, her family were thrown out on to the pavement by various landlords because they couldn't cope with her. She stole whatever she could, and reduced her family to being paupers because of her various drug treatments and goodness knows what else. Do you know why she's here? Her little brother prayed for her incessantly. He never gave up even when the mother herself gave up (albeit temporarily), weary of mind and body. The girl made it here—barely, actually. Her pimp shot her and she just had time to whisper, 'Jesus, forgive me' before she left the earth. Her brother is a preacher on earth. He's now 30 earthly years. I'm so proud of him. He's my son—well, grandson, a million times removed.

Why am I telling you all this? Because I want you to know that there is always hope for tomorrow, and for a better day. I don't know if I would have survived the onslaught experienced by the two families I have described, but I've noticed that God seems to know exactly how much you can take. Despite what you may think or feel, he never, ever gives up on his children. Night and day, heaven is filled with the sound of prayer for the earthly saints from angels and heavenly saints. If you could only hear it!

I know, I know. There are no easy answers, despite what the titles scream out from the bookshelves: *Quick Spiritual Steps for Perfect Families!* Situations won't always be resolved easily. It's an ongoing process, and, a lot of the time, it's a painful one. But rest assured, it's just for a while, a season—much like our time on earth.

The key is process. I'm not sure you know this, but God is as interested in our process of growth as in the final outcome. Think of the apostle Paul. Yes, he was a fiery one, but at the end of his life he could say with all equanimity, 'I have fought the good fight, I have finished the race, *I have kept the faith*' (2 Timothy 4:7). At the end of every challenge or situation, can the same thing be said of you? Don't get me wrong: there will be instances when our faith weakens and we grow weary in doing good. What I am talking about is a consistency in our faith that enables us to face challenges head-on. That is what pleases God.

I'll also tell you something that will prove an enormous help to all of you who are mothers and wives. I've had a lot of time to consider earthly matters from a heavenly perspective, and I find it incredible that human beings essentially make the same mistakes over and over again. King Solomon said, in one of his greatest moments of lucidity, that there was 'nothing new under the sun' (Ecclesiastes 1:9). Why do we always wait for things to get much, much worse before confronting the situation in front of us? Take the e situation of my son Cain. I should have known that Cain wouldn't let the Lord's indictment against his offering pass. He was always hot-tempered, always striving to do good and always by his own efforts. Maybe he thought that the plants—the offering of his own labour—would please God. After all, it's the thought that counts, right? Maybe he didn't realize how seriously God took the whole animal sacrifice thing. I don't know what he thought, but either way, God was not satisfied with his offering and made it known to him. Cain wasn't happy—at all. I think he was even angrier because the Lord revealed to him what was in his heart and he didn't like that one bit. God knew he was planning to kill his brother and told him as much: 'If you do what is right, will you not be accepted? But if you do not do what is right, sin is crouching at your door; it desires to have you, but you must master it' (Genesis 4:7).

Well, Cain didn't listen. He knew what he was going to do and nothing anyone said—not even God—would change his mind. So he persuaded Abel to go out into the field with him, and killed him while they were there.

I think I always knew what would happen, but I didn't want to say or do anything that would make matters worse between the two of them. You'd think I would have known better, but I was learning, and at great personal cost, the effects of sin on life. There are some reading this who know that something is not quite right with their child, or spouse, or another member of their extended family. Maybe your children are hanging around with the wrong 'sort'. Maybe your spouse is engaging in less-than-salubrious activities. Or maybe you yourself have developed a habit which, left unchecked, could metamorphose into a destructive one. I know, I know. It's easier to bury your head in the sand and tell yourself that it will go away. I understand that you don't want to make a fuss. I understand that you don't want to rock the boat. Believe me, I understand all that, but believe me too when I say that, further down the line, you *will* wish you had made a fuss. You *will* wish you had brought your head out of that sand and you will wish you had been honest with yourself about that habit.

We've been talking about strategies for survival but none of them would matter one jot if we forget about the most important one of all: communication. As you know, when I was on earth we didn't have family counsellors, parenting classes, marriage instruction manuals and Lord knows what else they're filling the libraries, bookshops and churches with nowadays. We just had ourselves and that was it. In many ways, it was easier. We were living in such close proximity with one another that nobody had a chance to become an island. Allow me to rephrase that: there were precious few opportunities to nurture humanity's ingrained desire to be selfish. It just wasn't possible. What 21st-century people call a 'biblical community' was normal everyday life to us. When people wanted to get married, the older generation pulled the engaged couple aside and mentored them on married life. When couples had disputes, the whole family was involved in the mediation process and, no, it wasn't called interference. The bottom line was that we communicated without making 'communication' the mystical buzzword that it has become these days.

Ongoing steps to family restoration

Restoration is an ongoing process, so stop looking for quick and easy answers. Think of it like this. We all have somewhere that we like to call our home, even if, in some cases, that 'home' is a cardboard box by the roadside. A house is an empty shell. It's the little touches that we add to the place that turn it into a home. And so it is with families. If we don't nurture each other, care for each other, encourage each other and learn to accept each other's faults, we will end up with a collection of individuals who just happen to be living with each other and no more. If we do work at it, we end up with a family.

For the single parent wondering where they fit in with this Christian Family Robinson scenario, I say, 'Wait a minute!' I'm not finished yet, and I certainly haven't forgotten you. There are many books and sources of help for single parents, especially single mothers, but I know that you can still feel left out of the whole Christian family business. You may feel that you don't measure up. And if you're a single mother and your children make Beelzebub look like the archangel Gabriel, then everything I've talked about is definitely for you. Remember, you are not alone. Anyway, chances are that your pastor's children are worse than yours.

Life is not easy. My escapade with the forbidden fruit has made sure of that. However, the good Lord in his mercy has given us the grace to conquer and work through life's challenges. A lot of the time, it feels like a bloodbath of an adventure; but a lot of other times, it will feel as if you're sailing on eagle's wings. But that's the Lord for you...

I've shared my sorrows, my joys and everything that Adam and I went through when Cain murdered Abel. Sure, there were times when we blamed ourselves. After all, didn't we spend time in Eden and have distinct recollections of how things could have been? Then again, we came to terms with the fact that Cain was full of self-motivated works from the beginning. He wanted to serve God on his own terms. As you and I know, that's sheer religiosity, and the Lord hates it. Whoever heard of the sheep going to the lion and saying, 'I know you're big and mighty but you're just going to have to do things my way and that's it.' The sheer effrontery of it! Well, that's how Cain appeared to God. The fact is that he wasn't willing to change or embrace the laws that God laid down, and that was his downfall. It was a bitter truth to swallow but Adam and I eventually managed it. We tried not to let it affect the other children and family members—we encouraged them not to speak evil of Cain—but neither did we forbid them from talking about the whole event. If you have children or family members in prison, or there is some terrible event or shameful secret in your life, don't let it enslave you. That would mean you had become a slave to fear, and the Lord has not given us timid spirits but the Holy Spirit, who is full of power, of love and unabashed boldness (2 Timothy 1:7). But all that means nothing if you do not allow the Lord to work through you. It will take a lot of courage. When you open up to people (not just anyone, though: use discernment) about your situation, you will be making yourself vulnerable, which is not a comfortable state. But that's because your human shield of protection is gone—and that is good, because it leaves you with no other choice but to rely on God. That's always the best thing to do.

There are no perfect families, only families that are being perfected—yes, even those with family members in prison. So your son or daughter is serving time for murder? Well, my son killed my other son. So someone in your family has accusations of rape against them? Well, I helped bring in a reign of evil called 'sin' and the whole earth has been living with its repercussions ever since. I urge you to hold your head higher and draw your strength from the Lord

2

Sarah: looking back on a lifetime

The Bible does me a great honour by listing me in the Hebrews 'hall of faith'. When I was on earth, I did not think I demonstrated enough faith in God's promise that Abraham and I would have a son together. Surely, the fact that I took matters into my own hands was a sign of my unbelief? It is only now, in heaven, that I realize the significance of God's promise. I am continually reminded of the Bible verse, 'Now we see but a poor reflection as in a mirror; then we shall see face to face. Now I know in part; then I shall know fully, even as I am fully known' (1 Corinthians 13:12). I guess wonders will never cease.

My father was Terah and my husband was Abram (as he was called before the Lord gave him another name—Abraham; of course, I was Sarai before the Lord made me Sarah). He was also my half-brother: we had different mothers. Don't gasp—we liked to keep things in the family in those days! We lived in a city called Ur of the Chaldeans. In due course, my father decided to move to Canaan, so he took his grandson, Lot, as well as Abram and me. In the event, we stopped off at a place called Haran, and decided that we would be better off there, so we stayed in Haran until Terah died. We thought we would live the rest of our lives in that place, but the Lord had other ideas. One day, he spoke to Abram and told him that he was to go a faraway land, and so off we went—Abram, Lot, myself, our livestock and servants, not really knowing where we were going. We had a sense of purpose, though, that we were on the right path. Abram trusted the Lord; I trusted my husband and our nephew; the servants and livestock trusted us. At the start of the journey, I was 66 and Abram was 75, young enough in the reckoning of those days, but, by today's standards, ancient.

In later years, I was often asked how Abram could up and leave without knowing where he was going. Well, the answer was very simple. He trusted the one he was following: God. He trusted as people down through history have trusted the same God and responded to his call with obedience. They probably didn't envision the road ahead and the many adventures they would face, but they trusted the Lord's faithfulness, believing that he would bring them through. That is exactly what Abram and I thought: the Lord called and we obeyed. Full stop.

People often wonder what it was like being married to Abraham, the first of the patriarchs, father of a nation. I don't know how best to answer that question but I will try. Everybody has moments of doubts on their faith journey. They experience seasons in their lives when they cannot help but cry out, 'I believe, Lord, but help me in my unbelief!' The only time my husband had those moments was when we were having difficulty conceiving a child. It wasn't that we weren't having much success in that area. We weren't having any success at all!

I knew Abram all my life, first as a brother, and second as his wife—and he gave me no end of adventure in both capacities. When we arrived in Canaan, the Lord made a promise to Abram: he said that he would give that land to Abram's offspring. I didn't think Abram had heard right. While I did not doubt the Lord's ability to give us our own child, the procreational process involved was another thing entirely. Exactly whose bodies would the Lord use to accomplish this feat? Certainly not mine or Abram's! But I kept my thoughts to myself and joined my husband in worshipping God at the altar he insisted on building, on every pivotal occasion when he heard God.

As we continued to travel, a famine struck the land, so we decided to go towards Egypt to wait it out. As we approached the country's borders, Abram grew scared and ordered me to tell the Egyptians that I was his sister (which was true in one sense) so that they wouldn't kill him to get at me, his 'beautiful wife'. I wondered where his loyalties lay then. It was all very well for him, but what would happen to me if someone took a fancy to me and decided they wanted to marry me? What was I supposed to do—go along with it? Well, I went along with the pretence and found myself in the pharaoh's harem. The man even gave Abram many gifts because of me, ostensibly to woo me and thank Abram for giving him such a precious gift: myself. All the while, I was seething inside.

Abram was a brilliant businessman with a heart that sought the Lord. When it came to making sound marital decisions, however, he could be the most obtuse person in the world. In his bid to protect himself from possible assassination by people who might have taken a shine to me, he neglected to think about me. By taking me up into his harem, Pharaoh could have done anything he wanted with me. The fact that I did not sleep with him is a testament to God's mercy. In fact, the Lord sent a plague on the royal household. At around the same time that Pharaoh took me to his harem, God gave him a dream in which he saw Abram and me joined together at the wrist by a cord. Then this cord was stretched as I was taken from Abram's side and put inside the harem. And in the dream, as I was being taken from Abram's side, the plague started in the royal household. Being someone of great wisdom, Pharaoh summoned Abram to explain why he had given his wife away to live in a harem, bringing a curse on the heads of innocent people. Pharaoh didn't wait for Abram's reply before sending us packing, escorted out of the country under armed guard. We laughed about that incident years later, but it wasn't funny when it happened. In fact, I found the whole thing very humiliating. I had somehow expected Abram to be ready to die to defend his wife's honour rather than lose her to a harem, but I guess he preferred to employ his business skills and use me as a bargaining tool instead.

It's never enough

Somebody once said that the one thing you desire but don't have is what you believe you will be judged on. If you have no work but yearn to be usefully employed, you will assume that everyone is judging you for not contributing to society. If you are unmarried but long for a husband or wife, then you will believe that your single status is what people will see when they meet you. If you are married yet unable to have children, in your mind it stands to reason that your childlessness will be all people notice about you. And if your children are not reproducing at a fast enough rate, it seems that you will never be a grandparent, leaving you at the mercy of the comments of your peers.

I was a married woman but I had yet to procreate and fill the earth. In my day, it was considered a truly shameful thing for women not to have children. They were our banner and pride, and we wore them like trophies. Of course, because Abram and I were not breeding, it was somehow my fault: I was the woman. No one pointed the finger of blame at Abram. And the Lord wasn't helping matters much. His periodic appearances to Abram, with assurances that we would indeed have a child, just rubbed salt into our open wound. After a while, I would hear these assurances and simply nod as if I really believed. But inside, I would smile scornfully and mutter, 'So you say!' Not that I fooled the Lord.

One day, some 24 years after the Lord first told Abram that we would have a child, we had visitors—strangers. I overheard them telling my husband that he would have a son round about the same time the following year. Now that had to be the greatest joke ever. First of all, by this time I was 90 and Abram was 99. Our body parts no longer defied gravity, and we weren't exactly intimate with each other, so exactly how this child would come about was still a mystery to me. But I kept my thoughts to myself and laughed in secret. Abram and I had argued over this subject so many times and finally laid it to rest—or so we thought. It only became an issue again when the Lord reminded us about it, which was annoyingly often. There was also the problem of Ishmael, Abram's son.

Ten years after we arrived in Canaan, we were still awaiting the grand entrance of our son, who would usher in a nation of people as numerous as the stars in heaven. Of course we had the memory of the covenant between the Lord and Abram, but still there was no child. Something had to give. I'd waited and waited and would probably have kept on waiting if Abram had had his way—which he didn't. I wanted a child and, since it wasn't forthcoming, I made use of the only opportunity available to me. I gave my servant girl, Hagar, to Abram (for purely procreational purposes, mind) so that she could have a child for me, as was our custom in those days. I hadn't bargained on the little madam getting ideas above her station when she realized she was pregnant. I would be sitting under a tree in the heat of the day and she would walk up and down in front of me, rubbing her stomach and making comments about how tiring pregnancy was and what a shame it was that some people wouldn't know about that, because they'd never been, and would in all likelihood never be, pregnant. Or she would shirk her duties on the pretext that she was feeling faint, so that Abram would order her to rest. He didn't want to lose what was probably his son and only heir—the child that she was carrying. And she carried on like this until I exploded to Abram about her attitude.

Ready as always to avoid household politics and uphold the peace, he told me to do anything I wanted to resolve the matter. Let's just say that I took the appropriate steps. In later years, I looked back at my behaviour towards that poor girl and cringed. There were days when I would wake up knowing exactly how to make her wish that she'd never been born, had never set foot in my household, much less set eyes on my husband, and had never seen my husband naked, let alone slept with him and carried his child. Her pregnancy was a stench to my nostrils, an eyesore to me and a daily reminder that she had succeeded where I had failed. And I was going to make her pay.

I didn't want to admit it to myself but I was directing my anger and disappointment with God and my husband towards that girl. She was an easy and vulnerable target. To be fair to myself, she wasn't exactly wise either. Flaunting her pregnancy at me wasn't the most sensible approach for a girl in her position. I was her mistress and I had complete control over her life. Did she really think that

Abram would choose her over me, just because she was carrying his offspring? What a deluded girl! In the end, I treated her so badly that she ran away. A day or so later, however, she came back, full of remorse and with a much better attitude. She started to tell me that she had had a visitation from God—but she was an Egyptian, so what did she know about the one true God?

I didn't listen to her. I wasn't interested. The truth was, I didn't really need her around. I could easily have got myself another maid. I could have done without the household servants sniggering behind my back at the saga of Abram, Hagar and myself, but Abram could not have coped with losing his child. When he had found out about Hagar running away, he had stayed out of my way for the whole day. When he did see me, he was painfully polite. I knew what he was doing: he was mourning the disappearance of his unborn child and, at the same, trying to shield me from the pain of his loss, out of respect for my feelings. I had no choice: I had to welcome Hagar back. If she hadn't come back, I would probably have gone to look for her myself, purely for my husband's sake—not mine.

I'm pretty certain that you gasped when you first read about Hagar, the servant girl who eventually gave my husband a son. The fact that it was common practice for wives to give their servants to their husbands for procreation still didn't make the situation easy. Hagar was young and I wasn't. Abram never said so, but I'm fairly certain he preferred her firm, unwrinkled body to mine. I knew of some instances where the servant girl had actually usurped the wife's role. It began with regular visits to the master's tent for straightforward procreation sex, but then the master would start talking about the servant girl—how wonderful she was, how brave she was and what a sweet little person she was. Sweet, indeed! The girl had probably been planning exactly how she would end up as wife number two from the moment she joined the household. That is why we often kept an eye on our maids. We were women ourselves and knew how cunning we could be.

Hagar was a constant reminder of what a fundamental mistake I made in giving her to my husband so that she would be pregnant for me. As it turned out, when she had the baby Ishmael, I couldn't stand Abram touching him, although I tried. The baby simply made me think of my failure to have children of my own.

All this happened 13 years before the visitors came to us and said that Abraham (the new name given to him by God) and I would have a child of our very own within a year. When they said that, I looked at Ishmael and just laughed to myself. I didn't get away with it, though. The Lord heard my disbelieving laughter and told me off. For what it's worth, I didn't disbelieve the strangers. I simply didn't know how the Lord would perform this miracle. But everything happened exactly as the Lord said it would.

Abraham and I had a lovely baby. I was 90 and Abraham was 100. Our son was called Isaac, meaning 'laughter', because his conception and birth circumstances made people laugh at the wonder of it all. But there was still one more thing I had to do.

One day, we had a party to celebrate our son's weaning, and I saw Hagar and her son Ishmael making fun of him. It was a step too far. As if it wasn't bad enough that those two were still living in my household and reminding me of all those years I wanted to forget, they dared to mock Isaac, the true heir of the nation that God had promised my husband. I wasn't standing for it. I told Abraham to get rid of the two of them. I didn't want to see them, hear them or have anything to do with them ever again. I only wanted my husband and my son close to me—no hangers-on and false claimants to the inheritance. Abraham was upset. Ishmael was also his son, he said. He couldn't just send him away. 'That's fine,' I said. 'Then Isaac and I will leave.' He didn't hesitate when I told him that. Early the next day, he sent mother and child packing into the desert. If you want to know what happened to them, read Genesis 21:14–21. This is my story, not Hagar's.

I admit that, for years, I was consumed with my desire to have children. If conceiving comes easily to you, then you won't know what it's like to want something so badly that you would do anything to get it, regardless of the consequences. The Lord had promised Abraham and me a son. I tried holding on and believing God, but it was very hard. After ten years of waiting and nothing happening, I took matters into my own hands. But when Hagar got pregnant, I was even more miserable. It would have been better for me to have left things as they were. At least I wouldn't have been tormented by the sight of her and her son. Even so, the Lord kept on visiting my husband and telling him that he would have a child with me. It took 25 years but the promise came through, even though my sanity was barely intact.

Why did the Lord take so long to fulfil his promise? I don't know, but I know that a day in heaven is like a thousand years on earth (2 Peter 3:8) so those 25 years probably seemed like no time at all to God. I also know that every single promise of God to his people does get fulfilled eventually. If you grimaced when you read that, I don't blame you. I did pretty much the same thing when I was on earth.

Those 25 years of waiting on God's promise were hard, but I have yet to find someone in heaven or on earth who was promised something by God and received it immediately. God often seems to use that waiting time to mould a person's character through trials and challenges. Now I'm in the presence of the Lord and although I have the benefit of 'Godsight', I still feel a little bit of sanctified annoyance when I think about Hagar. No doubt about it, she was my 'thorn in the flesh' (2 Corinthians 12:7). Everybody has one—and, thinking about it, we all need one, because through it God enables us to see ourselves the way we truly are. We can then turn to him for strength to make the necessary changes to our characters in areas where we are lacking. If I could live my life on earth again, I wouldn't spend it being jealous of a young girl and expending my energy on making her pay for a decision that I took. I don't know if I could have loved Ishmael, but I think I would have tried to like him, albeit through gritted teeth.

Over the centuries, this faith business has done a lot to confuse God's children, but there is no mystery to it. Faith is a simple trust in God that he will do as he has promised. The more you know him and his ways, the more your faith is strengthened. We didn't have the Bible in my day. We had faith in a God who pledged himself to us. It just so happens that he used the one thing I desired above all else to teach me about relying on him and trusting in him despite what my body was telling me. I mean, Abraham and I were steadily getting older and older and more decrepit of body. Funny how the Lord ensured that we were well and truly old and decrepit before giving us Isaac. I guess he wanted to make sure that we wouldn't gloat in our efforts but marvel at how such an event occurred in spite of our age.

I admit it: I was wildly jealous of Hagar. I know I sent her to my husband myself but I truly believed that I didn't have any choice. The Lord's periodic appearances to my husband bolstered our faith no end, but there were times when those visits seemed to mock our faith in him. I think my head believed that God would give us a child, but I just didn't know how. After a while, Hagar understood that under no circumstances were she and her son to come near my tent after a visitation from God. Their presence used to rile me no end. I'm sure you are well familiar with situations of senior employees who are so jealous of the rising star in their companies that they do whatever is necessary to stop the star from rising. Well, in her own way Hagar was a star, and she fought back the only way she knew how. I have to admit it, though: she was certainly a fighter. She had to be—look who she had for a mistress!

3

Leah: being a married single

Sometimes I think I should be on a daytime TV chat show. I don't know anyone else who's had to share a husband with her own sister and even had to bargain for sex with him using some stupid mandrake roots. But these are the depths to which I sank when Jacob came into my life.

I never ever thought that my life with him would turn out the way it did. Like most women in this book, I imagined that my married life would be one blissful dream. Instead I found myself in a nightmare of pain and unhappiness. Eventually, God did turn those seasons of ashes into coverings of beauty for me, but it wasn't easy—not by a long shot.

Being second best

Rachel was always the beautiful one. I was the one with 'the eyes'. Some people called my eyes delicate. I prefer to call them what they were: short-sighted and rather rheumy. Rachel was the one who got the marriage offers. I was the one who my father, Laban, was ready to palm off on the highest bidder. He didn't care who it was; he just wanted to make sure I was settled before Rachel. Many were the times I looked at Rachel and wondered what it was like to be her. People say she was so like our Aunt Rebekah, my father's sister, who married Isaac, Jacob's father. (Sarah did mention, in the previous chapter, how we liked to keep things in the family…)

Everybody knows my Aunt Rebekah. Even today, so many centuries later, in sermons and Bible study groups across the earth, people say, 'She was very beautiful' (Genesis 24:16), just as they say of Rachel, 'She was lovely in form, and beautiful' (Genesis 29:17). When I was on earth, I was more interested in my aunt's love story, because it gave me hope. My father liked to regale us with stories of how Eliezer, my grandfather-in-law's most trusted servant, came in search of a bride for my father-in-law, Isaac. Legend has it that an angel of the Lord directed Eliezer's steps straight to Rebekah and the rest, as they say, is biblical history. I hoped and prayed for the same. What I got was Jacob.

It is difficult for anyone who hasn't been in my sandals to understand what I went through with that man. Then again, unrequited love is not a new phenomenon and it will keep on happening until the end of all things—but oh, the pain of it! Knowing that I had a father who was as wily as far as money was concerned didn't make things easier. He even tried to con Eliezer when he came to ask for Aunt Rebekah's hand in marriage. He tried to pretend that he was watching out for his sister, but Eliezer wasn't fooled. He had a job to do and he made sure he left with the person he came for: Rebekah (Genesis 24:30, 55).

Some people say that my father only gave Jacob a taste of his own medicine. After all, Jacob did cheat his own brother Esau out of his inheritance. That was why he upped and left Beersheba to travel 400 miles to Haran, where we lived. It was either that or be killed by Esau. I don't know, and neither do I care. All I know is that Jacob appeared in my life and nothing was ever the same again.

I used to wonder what it was like to be beautiful and to be loved by someone as fiercely and as passionately as Jacob loved my sister Rachel, but I don't think I ever did understand or even experience the fullness of such a love. I was too busy fighting a fearsome battle of sexual and marital rights with Rachel. Looking back, I wish we had spent more of our time rejoicing in what we had—each other. If we had chosen to, we could have risen up above our circumstances. Yes, the circumstances were far from ideal but we could have spent a lot more energy trying to work things out, instead of engaging in our soul-destroying wars. And guess who enjoyed the full benefits of our battles? Jacob, of course! Rachel and I argued over sexual favours with our husband. We argued over children: who had them, who didn't and who deserved them. When I couldn't have any more children, I pushed my maid Zilpah towards Jacob so that she could have children for him (they were mine by default); and because Rachel initially couldn't have children, she pushed her maid Bilhah towards him as well, who also had children for him. It was ridiculous, and the only person who gained was Jacob, who had the dubious pleasure of having four women at his sexual disposal. I look back and cringe. How could Rachel and I have been so stupid?

I'm afraid I've started my story by jumping right into the nitty-gritty. It's just that I have so much to get off my chest. As women, we believe that marriage will somehow give us the contentment, peace and security that we need, and that it will remove that allegedly awful stigma of being 'single'. But I am here to tell you of a different kind of married life—the kind I went through; the kind that many, many married women know but are too afraid or emotionally scarred to talk about. This kind of married life is called being 'married single'. If you are one of those people, I pray that my story will encourage and strengthen you. I pray you will be reassured that you are not alone and, most importantly, that through my story you will encounter the grace of God and learn to depend on him as I had to do through extremely trying times.

Courtship? What courtship?

As I have already said, in my day we liked to keep things in the family, or kin, or clan, or whatever you want to call it. It made things 'easier' and, besides, it was better than being married to any of the heathens who lived all around us.

I remember the day Jacob was introduced to us. He was on the run from his twin brother, Esau. I told you earlier that he'd cheated Esau out of his inheritance and feared for his life. Did I also mention that Jacob means 'the deceiver'—or something very close to that? Anyway, I'm getting sidetracked. It's just that I would like you to know what I faced with Jacob, that deceiver *extraordinaire*.

Like I said, I remember when my father brought Jacob home. I also remember Jacob looking at Rachel. My heart sank because I knew that, once again, I would be in the way. Laban would certainly not agree to Rachel getting married before me, her older sister. Our custom dictated that the older sister got married before the younger one. That's the way life was—always had been, always would be. To be honest, I don't think Rachel had ever felt that I was in the way of her marital happiness, because no one had really yet caught her heart. We hadn't bargained on Jacob, the rollercoaster that came roaring into our lives, changing them for ever, as well as world history. I, for one, hadn't bargained on falling in love with him. Oh, stupid, stupid heart. Why did God give us one, anyway? When I was on earth, I often thought that life would be easier if we didn't have the capacity to love or feel any kind of emotion, but then I'm reminded of my children and the Father God's love for me and I'm brought back to my senses. I wouldn't swap the heartaches for anything in the world, excruciating as they were.

But that's all by the by. Jacob came, saw Rachel and fell in love. He asked for her hand in marriage a month later. Since he didn't have any money or any kind of offering for the bride-price, he agreed to work for my father for seven years. That was his bride-price. My father agreed, scarcely believing his good fortune. A free worker for seven years!

Seven years is a long time to wait when you're working to claim the hand of the one you love, but it didn't seem so for Jacob. He didn't mind. He saw Rachel every day. As far as he was concerned, time was of little consequence, so those seven years felt like a few days (Genesis 29:20). And what was I doing during those years?

Well, numbers had special meanings in our culture. Forty meant a very long time, and seven was the most complete and perfect number: the Lord created the world in six days and rested on the seventh. We lived in very close-knit communities, and everyone knew that Jacob was working for Rachel. It was like Aunt Rebekah's and Isaac's love story all over again. The fact that they met at a well, just like Rebekah and Isaac, was not lost on me either. It was the kind of love story I had prayed and hoped for, only it wasn't happening to me. It was happening to my beautiful sister; Rachel, the one with the lovely face and beautiful figure. I wanted to be a seven. I wanted to be complete and perfected in love and marriage, but it didn't happen.

In those seven years, I didn't have my own love story. The only suitors who came for me probably came more out of pity than anything else. I think they thought I would jump at the chance to be married to anyone, regardless of the unhappy consequences, just to escape the pitying glances and the awful burden of knowing that I was in the way of my sister's wedding. Pitying glances or no pitying glances, though, I refused to let my father dispose of me like that. But why did he not simply insist that I obey him? Well, I think he already had his own scheme in mind... Anyway, I put up with the snide comments about my age, my present and future career as a spinster and the comparisons between Rachel and me. But how I bled emotionally! I thought God didn't care, but he saw everything and actually used my circumstances to get me married off eventually.

And so it came to pass that, at the end of the seven years, Jacob asked for his bride. I quelled the rising fear in my heart, because I suspected that his love story wouldn't have his desired ending.

The honeymoon or cold light of day

Many people have criticized my father for deceiving Jacob. They say he had no right to do what he did. These people forget that Laban was also a father. During those seven years, he'd seen my tears. He saw my dampening hope as each year led into the next and my hopes of marital happiness decreased. Ever the business man, he also realized that he could be lumbered with a spinster elder daughter who would for ever negate her younger sister's chances of getting married. That meant he would be saddled with two spinster daughters to provide for, for the rest of their lives—hardly cost-effective. It was a daunting thought and my father didn't like it one little bit. He saw a chance to kill two birds with one stone, as it were, and went for it with the wily skill of the serpent in Eden.

In our part of the world, men and women celebrated weddings separately, just as still happens in many parts of the world today. At the end of the wedding celebrations, the bride (face hidden to protect her 'modesty') was escorted into the bridegroom's chambers—usually by the entire wedding party, but my father did the honours this time. And that was how I found myself as Jacob's bride and in his bed. Did I know what I was doing? Yes. Did Rachel know? Yes. Could we do anything about it? No. This time, we had to obey our father. It was a win-win situation, he said. Once Jacob found out that he'd married the wrong sister, there would be a lot of shouting, he would demand Rachel, and Laban would give him Rachel as his second wife. And weren't we happy to share the same husband, being sisters and all? I won't bother repeating Rachel's answer. God gave you an imagination. Use it.

Needless to say, everything happened exactly as Laban said it would. I was led to Jacob's chambers. We slept together and the next morning he expressed his utter shock at finding me in his bed. Once again, I'll leave you to imagine my feelings at this stage.

A strange thing happened to me during those tumultuous times. I learnt a lot about God, life and broken dreams. I learnt to rejoice in the midst of my pain and I learnt a lot about love. But most importantly, I learnt a lot about myself. I was a married woman but I was alone. I was married to a man who had no regard for me except as a sister, but Jacob didn't have any choice. We had to procreate, and procreate we did. I thank God that he saw my shame and pain and gave me my children. And these children became my joy in my tenure as a 'married single'.

I had four sons, and then that was it. They stopped coming, for a while—until the mandrake incident.

Marriage as a journey

We often think about life and the way we want it to be. While my married life started out on surreal terms, I was still optimistic about the future. So what if my husband was wildly in love with my sister? So what if, as time went on, the neighbours whispered and shook their heads sympathetically at Rachel: 'She saved Leah's face by sharing her beloved Jacob with her. Now the poor girl can't have children, and Leah's just churning them out. It doesn't seem right.'

There were times when I thought I didn't care about all this. 'I have my children,' I would tell myself. 'I am doing well'—and I really was doing well. But sometimes, and quite unexpectedly, the pain would come, toppling all the protective shields I'd built around my heart and slicing it in half.

The pain came at night-time, when I ached for a man's touch, and it came when I attended to the children. I needed some form of acknowledgment that I'd done something right, if only in the area of childbirth—something that Rachel hadn't been able to achieve. The pain came when I cooked, yearning to see my husband's eyes light up in appreciation of my culinary effort. It came when I thought I would die from loneliness, but most of all, it came whenever I turned round and saw the pain in my sister's eyes as she saw *my* children, *her* nephews. We would look at each other and our eyes would wonder at the mess otherwise known as our lives. Could we fix it? Did we want to fix it? I don't think either of us knew the answers to those questions. The only way we knew how to proceed was to fight for our corner and claim our territory, and we did that very well.

You know what I mean. Maybe your husband has had an affair or is having an affair. Maybe the love in your marriage has died. It simply petered out and you're both too tired to resuscitate it. Maybe you don't even want to resuscitate it. Whichever is your case, it doesn't matter. I know your story because I lived it on earth. The fact of the matter is that you're married but you live an entirely separate life from your husband's. But tell me this: isn't there some part of you (a small part, maybe) that still refuses to believe that this is the end? As tired as you are of flogging this dead horse, wouldn't you agree that maybe you want to try again one more time? You see, that same small part of me just wouldn't let me give up on my husband and my marriage, despite our strange circumstances.

I have known the depths of despair and the pits of shame. The worse time was when I traded mandrake roots with Rachel in exchange for sex with Jacob. Back in my day, we believed that this root could remove sterility, and we also used it—in small doses—for its soporific effects. I didn't believe I was revealing my desperation. I believed I was taking charge of my life. I desired my husband, I wanted him to desire me equally, and I also wanted to have more children for him. Breeding was the only advantage I had over my sister, and if trading in mandrake roots was the only way to get into my husband's bed, well, that was what I had to do. There—I've said it—and you can laugh all you want. But I would have you know that after the mandrake incident, I had three more children. I like to think that the Lord worked through this situation, and whatever you readers may think about my lack of dignity, I still enjoyed a few nights of passion with my husband. I can imagine some of you reading this and thinking, 'So I'm not the only one!'

As a woman, I couldn't divorce my husband. And even if women were allowed to divorce in my day, did I even want to divorce Jacob? It would be tantamount to admitting that I'd failed—again. There was no way I was going to let that happen. Then there was the shame and embarrassment that such action would bring to my family. Anyway, where could I go, and what about my children—if indeed Jacob would have allowed them to go with me? Was I supposed to drag them around like pots and pans until someone took pity on me and took me in? No, I had nowhere else to go. (Of course, I'm not suggesting that you should stay if your partner is beating or abusing you. If that is happening, do exactly what David did when Saul was trying to kill him: run to a place of safety!)

Did things ever get better between Rachel and me? Yes, but not until after the mandrake episode. Could God have saved me from all those painful experiences? Of course, but he chose not to. I like to think that he wanted me to learn absolute reliance on him and, in the process, to find out about myself. He could have found more delightful ways of doing it, but the greatest lessons are best learnt in the valley of despair. I've yet to meet anyone who has been through the toughest of times and not agreed with this in some measure.

How the going got better

In the end, life changed because we moved away. Jacob stayed in Haran for almost 20 years before the Lord told him to return to Canaan, the land of his father Isaac. Personally, I couldn't wait to leave. It was an opportunity for us to start afresh, somewhere new, away from the prying eyes of my father and everyone else familiar with my sorry life. I guess Rachel felt the same way. She now had a son, Joseph (yes, you know his story). My sons, of course, spearheaded the campaign to get rid of him, but it wasn't their fault! If Jacob had shown them a tenth of the love and affection he showed Rachel's sons, then the whole slavery-and-Egyptian-prison debacle would never have happened. And the effrontery of the boy himself, strutting about, telling all and sundry that he saw his brothers bowing down and worshipping him. Who did he think he was?

When we started on the journey to Canaan, I thought everything would start getting better immediately, but life has a way of catching up with you when you least expect it. We were camping by the Jabbok River, near Succoth. Jacob had just spent the night fighting a mysterious man, who had won by displacing Jacob's hip. Jacob said that the man had told him to change his name to Israel. Rachel and I knew he'd had an encounter with God. It seemed to be further confirmation that we were right to go to Canaan, so we were still looking forward to meeting Israel's family there. Then we got the news that Esau was coming towards us with 400 men, presumably to kill Israel—who had stolen Esau's birthright and inheritance 20 years previously.

Israel was terrified, understandably, so he did what any normal human being would do in the circumstances. He sent gifts ahead of us to Esau, and arranged our travelling line thus: the maids Bilhah, Zilpah and their children travelled in front, I followed after them with my own children, and Rachel and Joseph came last. The irony of this travelling arrangement was not lost on me. In the event of any trouble, it was clear that Rachel and Joseph would have ample time to flee. That hurt. What about my children? Were they of less value than Rachel's? I'm telling you all this so that you understand the situations that faced me constantly. It seemed that every time I made a decision to act lovingly towards my sister and try to kill the bitterness poisoning my marriage, something else would come up and shake my will—like the time, after we had settled in Canaan, when my only daughter, Dinah, was raped. Just thinking about it now fills me with fury because once again my children bore the brunt of the troubled situation.

That day had started like any other. Dinah went to see some friends, but she didn't come back. Hamor, the prince of Shechem in Canaan, had taken a fancy to her, raped her and then decided he was madly in love with her and wanted to marry her. He had Dinah holed up in his tent, effectively a prisoner. Every mother has dreams for her daughter's marriage. Hamor crushed the dreams I had for my daughter. And he had the cheek to come to my husband and ask for her hand in marriage. Obviously no one was going to want her after what he'd done, but were we supposed to be grateful that he had declared undying love for her? Once again, I cried out to the Lord for wisdom and begged for his protection and mercy over my children. Rachel was a source of strength to me during those terrible days. No matter what had happened between us, Dinah was still her niece and I was still her sister.

My sons decided to avenge their sister. They gave Hamor and his father fictitious demands to fulfil before they would release their sister in marriage and, like fools, both Hamor and his father fell for it. Levi and Simeon went on the rampage after that. They went to the town and rescued Dinah, but not before slaughtering every man there. Then they plundered the town. It was a dreadful time. We were in fear for our lives. Suppose the neighbouring tribes decided to avenge what my boys had done? There was nothing for it but to move again, to Bethlehem, but this time I had come to terms with my lot in life. I realized that it would always consist of thorns and thistles. There would always be challenges, struggles and strife, and it was up to me to decide how I faced them all. Dinah's rape and the way it drew my sister and I closer together had caused me to re-evaluate my life: I accepted the status quo with Rachel and even accepted the fact that I would never be number one in Jacob's life—finally.

It wasn't so bad after all

My sister died in childbirth on our way to Bethlehem. Her son, my nephew, was called Benjamin. I find it hard to describe my feelings in the months and years that followed. Israel was never the same after she died, and neither was I. I mourned the fact that we had spent most of her life fighting and bickering over matters that suddenly didn't seem so important, now that she was gone. I missed her terribly. Whatever had happened between us, we were still blood relatives. I missed having someone to gripe at regarding our children and mutual husband. I missed her warm smile and beautiful face. I found myself pinpointing all the things I would do differently if she was around. I was there when she breathed her last and I sobbed as if my heart would break.

Israel was desolate. He wouldn't let anyone comfort him but instead drew Joseph and Benjamin, the newborn child, close to him. I didn't begrudge his behaviour this time. I'd learnt from the past, when my grudges against him hadn't brought me joy, but only more heartache. I was tired of having an aching heart. But how I ached for him! If I could have brought Rachel back to life just to lift the pain from Israel's heart, I would have done. I think I finally understood what the Lord had been trying to teach me all those years—that love is not self-seeking (1 Corinthians 13:5). For the first time, I wasn't comparing myself to Rachel or bemoaning my lot in life, and I wasn't going to use her death to advance my own interest. My concern was for Israel and how to make his pain easier to bear, so I grieved with him. He'd not only lost his wife but also his best friend. Now I endeavoured to be his helpmate, something I should have done more than 20 years earlier but had neglected because I was too busy scoring points against Rachel and thinking about myself, my needs and my loneliness. What a waste!

I know that some women reading this will shake their heads, perhaps in tears, and say, 'But I can't move on. I cannot forgive. I'm hurt. Too much has happened. You don't understand. I am alone. I am married only in name.' I hear you and I would never trivialize your circumstance by giving you glib answers. Being a 'married single' is difficult. You've just read my story, so you know that I understand something of where you're coming from. Please hear me out. The process of regeneration and reconciliation may be long and painful, but if you trust in the Lord, even when everything looks absolutely hopeless, I know he will transform the situation for you. You've seen how he changed my heart towards my husband. My circumstances hadn't changed, my husband still didn't love me, but somehow none of it mattered so much, because I decided to be obedient to the Lord and honour my marriage vows of faithful love and service.

It took a lot of courage for me to lay down my desires and take the first steps towards reconciliation. I realized that Jacob would never have taken that first step himself, for he never fully recovered from Rachel's death. Of course, there was always the chance that I would be rebuffed, but I was determined to do right by God. Over time, although he did not look at me as tenderly as he used to look at Rachel, I did see something akin to appreciation in his eyes—and that was fine with me.

And so ends my story. I am telling you this to give hope to all of you who have suffered or are suffering like I did, to let you know that your sojourn as a 'married single' is not for ever. It is only for a

4

Zipporah: Moses and mixed marriages

The Bible says that there is nothing new under the sun (Ecclesiastes 1:9). How true! Every generation thinks they are the first to witness or be a part of something, however good or evil that thing is—like this insane fear of foreigners, or 'immigrants', as you people like to call them. Consider here the words of the new king of Egypt: 'The Israelites have become much too numerous for us. Come, we must deal shrewdly with them or they will become even more numerous and, if war breaks out, will join our enemies, fight against us and leave the country' (Exodus 1:10). The new king failed to realize something that leaders on earth today still have to grasp: 'But the more they were oppressed, the more they multiplied and spread; so the Egyptians came to dread the Israelites and worked them ruthlessly' (Exodus 1:12–13). This is so true: whenever we fear something, we try to bring it under our control. The Israelites threatened the Egyptians and the Egyptians enslaved them.

When God created the earth, he provided more than enough resources to go round, but when I look at your recent history—the Holocaust, Rwanda, Darfur, the Balkans war and all the other conflict situations around the world in your day—I cannot help but wonder why humans have such a selfish desire to control everything and share nothing. It is this evil desire that is the root of war, all wars. We might dress it up as an ethnic or nationalist issue but ultimately it comes down to somebody's desire to keep all he or she has and prevent others from sharing it. It is also easy to blame others who do not belong to the same culture as you for everything that has gone wrong in your life, community, nation or even the whole world. But enough of that. You didn't buy this book to read a treatise on war and preventative diplomacy, even if I must admit to having outstanding skills in those areas!

Moses, my husband, was a Hebrew and I was a Midianite. Midianites were actually descendants of Midian, the fourth son of Abraham and his second wife, Keturah. It was Abraham himself who gave Keturah's sons his blessing and told them to go eastward (to modern-day Arabia) and multiply, which they did with obvious relish. As a Hebrew, Moses was a descendant of Abraham through Isaac, so Moses and I were not very different after all, just as you and every other person on earth are not very different from each other. We are all descendants of Adam and Eve. That fact alone should stop us looking suspiciously at each other's differences and instead enable us to rejoice in them. How boring life would be if we were all the same!

Some women spend their lives wishing their husbands, family, friends and children were 'perfect' according to their own standards. My philosophy is very simple: if your husband, children, family and friends were perfect, you would have nothing to moan about to your friends, family, children and husband! Let's face it, it's those very 'imperfections' or differences that can bring laughter into our lives. They also challenge us as individuals and force us to grow in areas of our character that we would otherwise never develop. Furthermore, if everybody around you was perfect, you would feel very imperfect in comparison to them. So, let's spend our time appreciating God's handiwork on earth and less time harping on our differences—or on how our cultures are being 'diluted' by others.

As I have said before, we are all descended from Eve. As we travelled to different corners of the earth, our bodies started adjusting to the different climatic conditions. It was only natural that different cultures, languages and skin shades would develop. These developments have taken thousands and thousands of years to occur, yet inside we're still the same: brothers and sisters. I am disturbed by the intolerance and prejudice that you people on earth are still showing to those who are different on the surface. It reminds me of my time on earth and some of the challenges I faced with Moses' people. And if it disturbs me, you can bet your sweet shekel that it grieves the Lord even more.

To be honest, the first time I saw Moses I didn't even know what I thought of him. My father thought it would be a good idea for me to marry him, so I did. You see, when I was a little girl, I had the usual kind of dreams. I wanted to get married, settle down, have children and live out the rest of my life in marital bliss. In my day, that was it. Yes, women did do other things, but mostly, getting married and breeding was all there was. So I had these wonderful dreams, but what I got was a Hebrew husband and a whole load of stress from his Hebrew people, who had issues with the fact that I was a Midianite. And get this: they only had issues with my Midianite self when they had something to complain about to Moses—which was pretty much all the time.

In addition, I had to contend with the fact that God chose to reveal himself to the Hebrews (and, by default, the whole human race) through my husband Moses. Then there were the ten plagues, the coming out of Egypt and the wanderings in the wilderness. The whole experience wasn't exactly a picnic but we learnt a lot about ourselves, about God and the way he wanted us to follow him. I'll come to that later, but I'll say this here and now: all those rules and regulations known as the Law took some getting used to.

Like I was saying about Moses, I didn't think much about the fact that he was Hebrew. If my father thought he was good enough for me, it wasn't right for me to use up energy doubting his choice. Having said that, though, I felt that Moses had some serious issues on his mind. For starters, he was very hung up on the fact that, as a child and young man, he enjoyed the luxuries of the Egyptian king's palace while his people suffered and slaved outside in the desert sun. I didn't really understand his frustration, to be honest. After all, why beat yourself up about something you cannot change? But then again, I suppose I'd never gone through what Moses experienced. I don't know what it's like to see your people subjugated and humiliated simply because somebody decided they were some kind of threat. I have to admit that there were times when I thought Moses should stop thinking about himself—especially about the fact that he'd killed someone—and focus on the task of living. He had left Egypt far behind; he was settled in Midian with a job, a wife and a family. Why harp on about the past? He couldn't change it, and while I wasn't happy about the fact that my husband was a murderer, I realized that some things were better left where they belonged—in the past.

The burning bush experience

I admit it: I thought Moses had lost his mind when he came home that day, telling me about the burning bush. I didn't really take much notice until he began talking about going back to Egypt. Then I started to listen. I didn't want to go to Egypt. I liked my life in Midian the way it was. I'd always known relative freedom and I'd heard stories from other travellers and from Moses himself about the condition of the Hebrews in Egypt. What made him think I wanted to be a part of that? And all that stuff about being God's spokesman and his staff turning into a snake? Spare me, please! And I won't lie, I was also worried about how his people would receive our family—me in particular. Did I have the energy to learn a whole new way of life, new words and customs? And what about my relatives? Was I supposed to bid goodbye to all I'd ever known? I didn't know what to think.

Then I thought about the man I married. No, he hadn't gone mad. He was prone to melancholy but definitely not madness. I remembered the stories he would tell me about the Hebrew God—how he was so big that he couldn't be contained on earth, yet, if asked, would come to dwell in the hearts of men and women. I thought about these stories—my husband believed them whole-heartedly—and I came to the conclusion that my place was with my

Moses, even if he decided to go to the ends of the earth. Yes, I would follow him even to Egypt because he was obeying his God. Of course, I wished his God had chosen somewhere closer to my own people, like Midian, but he hadn't. Despite my fears about not fitting in with the Hebrews and my nightmares about living in slavery, I resolved to support my husband, no matter what. I was actually happy that Moses would be able to see his own family again—his brother Aaron and his sister Miriam. I knew he yearned for them and, as much as he loved my father and the rest of my people, his heart belonged with his own. As it turned out, I didn't follow him all the way to Egypt, as he decided that I would be better off with my father, so he sent me back to Midian! So much for my worrying…

It wasn't easy being me

At times, being Moses' wife was a real drag. At other times, it was just a lonely and frightening experience. There were days when I didn't think Moses would survive the continuous onslaught of the people against him. I wasn't there when he faced Pharaoh on his own, asking him to let the Israelites go into the wilderness to worship the Lord, but how I wish I had been! The children and I stayed in Midian and heard of the miracles and the plagues from travellers. I busied myself with crying and praying to his God, whom I'd come to believe in, to protect my husband. It is no secret that Moses wasn't the most articulate person in the world. He was very aware of his weaknesses and although I knew the Lord had promised to protect Moses and give him the words to speak, and had even nominated Aaron as his spokesman, I couldn't help but be concerned for him all the time he was in Egypt. He was, after all, my husband. I felt proud every time I heard dramatic reports of what the Lord was doing through him to the Egyptians, but I feared for him as well. And I found that I missed him when he was away, terribly.

Life is so strange. You marry someone and make assumptions about how you will live out the rest of your lives together, but then you realize that God has other ideas. In many ways, Moses was just an ordinary man, but the Lord equipped him for the task of leading his people out of Egypt and transformed him into a great leader. During that process, we learnt a lot about each other and about the people God called him to lead. It wasn't an easy process, and I took the constant attacks on him very personally. He was for ever praying and pleading with the Lord not to exterminate the Israelites because of their stubbornness. If he wasn't doing that, he was settling their disputes. He was constantly looking over his shoulder, wondering when they would attack him, and all the time he was just trying to serve God and do what the Lord wanted. That was the hardest thing to bear. I suppose this is why I have a special compassion for women whose husbands are in ministry today.

We didn't have telephones, e-mail, internet, fax machines, the post, bleepers and satellite dishes in those days, but people still knew where to get hold of Moses and me. Our tent was right there in the camp with the people, so we couldn't hide. We had a steady and constant stream of visitors, all day and often all night. My concern was not for myself. It was for my husband, because those visitors drained him emotionally and physically. I was the perfect hostess, with the ability to disappear when not needed—which was most of the time. Yet people wanted to get close to me, because I had the insider's view on Moses and they thought I could perhaps tell them what was coming next. Other people wanted to get close to me because they'd decided it was a good idea for me to 'lead the women'—whatever that meant—which I wasn't interested in doing. I just wanted my husband and children and the life we had had in Midian, when life was predictable and stable.

I was willing to accept my new way of life, but I wasn't adjusting at the speed that some people wanted. I also believed that they wanted me to conform to their expectations of me. They weren't to know that I was still trying to figure it out myself. And then there were the precious people whom God sent to encourage me when I was down, strengthen me when I was convinced I would die from frustration, and rejoice with me in the good times. Yes, God does take care of his own. If you're a woman with a husband in the ministry, take heed of my words: ask the Lord to surround you with people who see you as an individual in your own right and treat you like a person, not an appendage to your husband. Believe me, once the Lord sends such people to you, you will wonder how you ever managed without them. No more wondering whom to trust!

For those times when the stress of sharing my husband with so many people proved to be too much, I turned to my inner circle, knowing that anything I shared with them stayed with them. I'm sure those of you in similar situations understand the value of such people—priceless, absolutely priceless!

The ministry—my husband's mistress

We were in the wilderness for about 42 years, although it felt more like 420. At each level of the ministry came new challenges. That's the way life goes. My father took me and my two sons to Moses a few months after he had led the Israelites out of Egypt. They were camped at Mount Sinai. Any thoughts I had had about spending some quality time with Moses and our sons as a family were duly crushed as Aaron and the leaders of Israel came to share a meal with him. My father was included as an honoured guest. The next day, Moses was settling disputes from dawn to dusk and I was left to acquaint myself with our new home and extended family. Thank God for my father, who advised Moses on the importance of delegation. And this is what all who are ministers' wives should impress upon their husbands. He is only one man, and he cannot do everything. Contrary to what he might think, the ministry or church, or whoever is his 'mistress', will not collapse without him. If he dies, the church will get itself another leader and you'll be left without a husband, wondering what it was all for. I know that sounds harsh, but a little harsh reality never killed anyone.

I really thank God for those years in Midian when I'd had my husband to myself. At least he was able to be with our sons then— Gershom and Eliezer. I don't know what I would have done if that hadn't been the case. I guess my feelings would probably mirror yours, all those of you whose husbands constantly put the needs of the congregation or ministry before your family's needs. He doesn't have the time to take little Emily to school but would drop everything if a congregation member's child broke a toenail (a slight exaggeration, perhaps, but I think you know what I mean). Or maybe your husband is a travelling evangelist. He's out on the road 40 weeks of the year and you're left to raise the children on your own. You feel like a single mother, and you're resenting the 'ministry mistress' that's taking your husband away from you. As if that wasn't enough, guilt starts setting in because you're supposed to be a good Christian wife and you just know that you shouldn't be having these most unChristian feelings. Well, call those feelings what you like, you can't escape or ignore them. Trust me, I know.

If I were you, I would pick an appropriate time to discuss it with your spouse, in the hope that the two of you will come to some kind of agreement. Whatever you do, though, don't give your husband an ultimatum—you know, the 'ministry or me' question. Otherwise, you might end up coping with more than you bargained for. Ask the Lord, and the trustworthy people with whom he has surrounded you, for wisdom.

Moses' ministry was threefold: getting the Israelites out of Egypt, revealing God to them through the Law, and leading them into Canaan. At each stage of the ministry, just when I thought I was getting it all together, something would happen and I would have to go face down before the Lord. Whatever you might want to say about the Lord, being with him is never a boring exercise. Excruciating sometimes, glorious at other times, but never boring.

Moses and I couldn't really separate our personal lives from the 'ministry' because God designed it that way. His brother Aaron was his spokesman and the high priest, and of course there was Miriam.

She was a prophetess in her own right, so we were all in 'ministry' together. When things were going great, relations were fine between Moses, myself and the other two. But when things got ugly, they got really ugly. I remember the time when Moses went up Mount Sinai to receive the Ten Commandments. The whole nation of Israel was assembled at the bottom of the mountain as requested by the Lord. When Moses didn't come down from the mountain quickly enough, everyone started getting twitchy and the griping started. They wanted to know where Moses was and what he was doing. Wasn't it time he came back? What were they meant to do in the meantime? And what about this God they were supposed to worship but couldn't really see? Wouldn't it be better to have something the whole camp could focus on? Wasn't this God just another of the sort they'd worshipped in Egypt? They went on at Aaron until he gave in and made them a golden calf, moulded from the jewellery that they gave him.

I couldn't watch. All I could think of was Moses and how much I wanted him to come back down from the mountain. And he did come down eventually, his heart full of excitement at everything the Lord had shared with him on the summit. He even had stone tablets covered with God's own writing, instructing them on the way to live! His exhilaration didn't last long, though. His disappointment at the sight that greeted him made him smash the stone tablets in righteous anger. The people had gone crazy—laughing and drinking and indulging in those horrible sexual practices that had characterized their 400 or so years in Egypt.

Moses didn't waste any time. First he stood at the entrance to the camp and asked those on his side to come and join him. Only the Levites—the priests—came. Then he told the Levites to go and kill everyone who had worshipped the calf, which they did. That day, three thousand people died by the sword. And then, the Lord sent a plague that killed even more people. That was hard. I pray that you never face such a situation. I will never forget the grief of those who were left—like a presence that at times threatened to overwhelm us. I feared for my husband's and children's lives, too.

What if the people decided to turn on us? I felt like a politician's wife during a coup and the stench of the bodies in the wilderness sun did not make me feel any better. I bore the snide remarks and poisonous darts that were sent my way afterwards, because of what my husband had supposedly done. Like all things, it eventually passed. At times, though, the memory of those rotting bodies in the sun flits through my mind.

During this time, I also had to confront my unsettling feelings towards God. Moses had told me that the Lord had chosen the Hebrews to be his own special people and that he would fight their battles for them. Sending the plagues on the Egyptians I could understand, because they were a threat to the Hebrews, but destroying his own people to discipline them was a lot harder for me to accept. From that moment I feared God, even as Moses was drawing into a more intimate relationship with him.

Other experiences were dreadful in different ways—like the time Miriam and Aaron decided to turn on me for being a Midianite (Numbers 12:1–15). Attacks on Moses' leadership qualities were bearable because they were attacks on his professional credibility, but when the attacks became personal, well, they hurt. The Lord came to my defence and punished Miriam by giving her a skin disease and banishing her from the camp for seven days while her skin cleared up. That made things just a tad uncomfortable between us, as you can imagine. There was also the time when Aaron lost two of his sons because they failed to follow God's instructions about the burning of incense in the tabernacle (Numbers 3:2–4). My heart went out to him, despite our differences over the years. I was a mother myself, after all.

But one of the most difficult and frightening times was when Korah led a rebellion against Moses with about 250 other prominent leaders of Israel (Numbers 16). The charges against Moses were the same as usual: he wasn't the only one who could speak to God directly, so why was he lording it over them, and so on and so forth?

This time, Moses had had enough. He summoned his accusers and their supporters together and told them to appear before the

Lord with their incense. Korah went one stage further and stirred up everyone against Moses and Aaron. So now, *everyone* stood at the entrance of the tabernacle. The Lord was so angry that he threatened to annihilate them all. Moses, ever the intercessor, asked the Lord not to punish the whole nation for the sin of one man. God relented, and that day, Korah, Dathan and Abiram (the ringleaders) and their wives and children were swallowed up in an earthquake. I heard the almighty roar of the earth when it opened. I heard the people's screams as they were buried alive. But that wasn't all: the Lord also sent a fire that burned up Korah's 250 supporters. That day was a very terrible day. When I think of the smell of 250 burning humans and how nobody had the courage to move away from the scene for fear of antagonizing the Lord even further, I have to lift up my hands in awe and trembling fear. Like most of the people, I was asking myself: 'Who is this God we are following?'

The very next day, though, the nation gathered against Aaron and Moses and accused them of killing Korah and his people. I stayed in the tent with Miriam and the children and just prayed for the Lord to deliver us, which he did. He sent a plague among the people, which Aaron and Moses tried to stop by interceding for them. 14,700 people still died. For days and weeks after that, I experienced many feelings: fear, confusion and, above all, guilt, for I truly believed I had the blood of 15,000 people on my hands.

I didn't understand it then, but all those acts from God were to show the Israelites how valiantly he fights for his anointed. He viewed any attack on Moses and Aaron as a personal attack on himself. In fact, any time the people rose up against Moses and consequently God, they got seriously toasted by his anger. We lived in exceptional times, when graphic displays of God's power were needed so that the Israelites would learn to fear and love God in equal measure. They cannot be compared with today's usual church or ministry hassles! But if you are in ministry, you will come across people like those that Moses and I encountered during our sojourn in the wilderness. Do the same as Moses: pray for those people and let the Lord fight your battles. He might not do the same spectacular acts that he did while we were out in the wilderness, but his heart is still the same.

My memories of those wandering years aren't all bad. There were some wonderful times as well: my favourite was when the whole nation gathered together to build the tabernacle of the Lord. That was something else! I wish you could have seen it. The people gave so much towards its construction that in the end we had to beg them to stop. And the thanksgiving party, when the tabernacle was eventually finished, had to be seen to be believed.

Having a vision and living a vision aren't the same thing

The Bible says that the Lord's people are destroyed from lack of knowledge (Hosea 4:6). That is so true. If you and your husband are in ministry, you will come into contact with all kinds of people. There are those who see the ministry God has given you and will assist you in accomplishing that vision because they believe in it. There are people who do not have any ideas, but simply 'go with the flow'. It is not always a good idea to have such people with you because they lack a clear definition of their purpose in your ministry. They are like shifting sand or windblown waves. And then there are people who recognize the vision the Lord has given you but are not willing to 'cross the Red Sea' with you so that you can get there. They call themselves the 'voice of reason' but they are really the emissaries of fear and discouragement. Do not at any time confuse these people with the voice of legitimate concerns, as legitimate concerns are easily addressed. It is relatively easy to tell the difference between the two. Legitimate concerns encourage people to venture into the unknown, albeit with caution and faith. Fear and discouragement seek to destroy all hope, always, and must be attacked and conquered.

By the way, can you tell me the names of the ten other spies, as well as Joshua and Caleb, who were sent to survey Canaan? I thought not. Most other people can't recall their names either. Whatever vision the Lord has given you for your ministry, rest assured that it will always be bigger than you. That way, you can't count on getting the glory when it is fulfilled. You can also be sure that you will have to slay giants (although probably not literally) to get what is promised to you, and you can be doubly assured that you will need other people's help—so that you cannot boast about how you did it yourself. That, my dears, is the Lord's way. And so it was with Caleb, Joshua and the other ten spies who were sent to Canaan. They came back laden with fruits and produce, the likes of which we had never seen before. They also came back with glorious reports of the land the Lord was giving us, but they ended by telling us that it would be impossible to conquer it. The land was inhabited by giants, they said.

Only Caleb and Joshua argued otherwise. 'Is anything impossible for God?' they asked. 'Surely he has promised us the victory, so let's go in and take what is promised to us,' they said. But the nation of Israel wasn't listening. It was easier to listen to ten 'reasonable' men than two rather excited ones. Joshua, incidentally, was Moses' assistant, so of course he would take Moses' side!

Then the attacks started again. They should have died in Egypt. They were doomed to eat manna for ever. What would happen to them in the desert? Were they supposed just to roam around while waiting for their enemies to be kind enough to allow them into this land? And by the way, it didn't look as if they were going anywhere in particular, as Moses and Aaron kept them walking around the desert in circles. Oh, to be back in Egypt! Some people started talking of stoning Caleb and Joshua. Others talked about choosing someone to lead them all back to Egypt. As usual, I stayed behind the scenes in my tent, praying. I'd learnt from Moses. He prayed incessantly and, having seen God work through him and for him, I knew that it was the only reasonable thing to do. So I prayed with Miriam, my inner circle of friends, and my sons.

And then the Lord spoke. He was angry. He was fed up with his people. Nothing he did was good enough. After all his brilliant acts, he was still having to prove himself to his chosen nation. When would they learn? Maybe he should just wipe them out and choose another nation for himself. Moses wept, begged and pleaded with the Lord. The people were foolish, he said. They didn't know any better. He begged the Lord to spare them. Besides, what was the point of bringing them out of Egypt, saving them with great miracles and then exterminating them in the wilderness? God would be the mockery of his enemies. Eventually, the Lord relented. Fine, he said, but because of their disobedience and lack of trust, the people would roam in the wilderness for 40 years—a year for each day the spies were away in Canaan. At the end of the 40 years, the generation of people that had disobeyed God would be dead and their children would go into the land. And then, just so that they knew he was serious, he struck the ten spies who had incited the rebellion against him with a plague.

When the Israelites heard what the Lord had said, there was much sorrow. They woke up early the next day and decided that they would indeed take Canaan. They had learnt their lesson, they said. They were ready to claim their inheritance just as the Lord promised. Moses cautioned them against it but they didn't listen. They pressed ahead and were roundly beaten and chased away by the Amalekites and the Canaanites.

If you and your spouse are in ministry, you will experience seasons just like this one. Perhaps you want to take your work to a new level, as the Lord has revealed it to you, but all you are encountering is resistance. You're dejected and discouraged and even doubting what the Lord has told you. Take heart from my husband's ministry and strengthen yourself in the Lord. In every situation, his first instinct was to go to God. It was his lifetime's habit. He always spoke with God. That was why God called him his friend and why he would get incensed every time the Israelites spoke against Moses. Cultivate the habit of speaking with God, as you would with a friend. It is not rocket science, nor is it a mystical experience reserved for the especially righteous. As long as you have given your heart to God, you have his Holy Spirit, your Counsellor,

Friend and Advocate, living in you. Cultivate a relationship with him, and I guarantee that you will never feel lonely or afraid again.

5

Deborah: fighting wars and leading men

Deborah means 'bee'. Down the centuries, I have been called many things: judge, wife, prophetess—and I was indeed all those things—but I have never been called a bee. It's not a description commonly associated with a female judge—even if some of my judgments did sting—and a woman who marched with her men to battle.

Those were exciting, if uncertain, years. We spent a lot of our time hiding from our oppressors, cowering under their rule or engaging in gruesome battles. When I think back to my life on earth, I feel almost as if I lived someone else's life, not mine, because I can barely believe some of the things I did. Did I really stand in the midst of a battle, surrounded by hundreds of men, screaming, 'March on! The Lord is our strength!' When I had got through an event like that, I would look back and ask myself, 'What was I thinking?'

Thousands of years have passed since I was on earth but people still marvel at the fact that I was the only female judge to rule over Israel. A lot of explanations have been offered: that there weren't many men left in the villages of Israel, so God was forced to use a female; or that I somehow 'rose' out of Israel, that the people did not have any choice but to choose me. The real reason was simply that I was available and God chose to use me. For that I was thankful, although I didn't feel like being thankful all the time as the combination of being prophetess and judge could be rather taxing. God's people used to drive me mad with their squabbling. You wouldn't believe the disputes I had to resolve. I used to hold court under the Tree of Deborah in Ephraim. The most common arguments were inevitably about money, land or marriages. A lot of the time, they were about all three. From what I can see on earth today, it seems that nothing has changed on that score.

I had moments of laughter, though. There was a man who came to me, saying that he was a poor man who had given his livestock to the temple as the Lord commanded. Now, he wanted his offering back, because when he came home from the temple he discovered that raiders had stolen his remaining animals. God didn't need his livestock, he said. God had plenty: he was the Creator. As for him, he was a poor man. Could I ask the temple priest to return his livestock to him? My raucous laughter in response to the man could be heard all the way to Jerusalem. However, people were so moved—by laughter—at his story that he left the court with more animals than he could manage. It was such moments that made my position so pleasing. After a hard day of settling disputes, I would go home to Lappidoth, my husband, and manage my household. As you can see, women have always had two jobs: the day job and the evening job of being mother and wife.

In those days, our lives were rather matter-of-fact. We woke up and faced the day's challenges, be they war, kidnappings, massacres, weddings or whatever drama came along. We had a resilience shaped by a social environment that prided family honour and service to the nation above all else. It had to be that way, otherwise we wouldn't have survived the times. Because our enemies constantly surrounded us, we had to show them our strength in visible and demonstrative ways, or they would subjugate us. When we were living in accordance with God's laws, he fought our battles and gave us incredible victories, but when we turned away from him and embraced the lifestyle of the heathens around us, disaster usually followed. No wonder God gave us over to King Jabin of Hazor, one of the kings of Canaan who ruled over us! We didn't practise God's laws; we were more interested in the Canaanites' way of life, which, seen from afar, was more exciting than the seemingly prudish and impossible 'to do' list that made up the Law. 'You want to live like the Canaanites?' God asked us. 'Well, fine! I've given you over to them. Let them rule over you and we'll see how much you like that!' Well, we didn't like it at all, and we cried out to the Lord for deliverance again and again.

A woman's job

The commander-in-chief of Jabin's army was Sisera, a man who had 900 iron chariots (Judges 4:3). Israel supposedly had 40,000 warriors, yet our army was as weak as if they had not a single shield or spear among them (Judges 5:8). We were a sorry nation, at the mercy of this man who ruthlessly oppressed us for 20 years. We knew the stories of how God had delivered our ancestors out of Egypt and parted the Red Sea for them to cross into Canaan. We were enthralled by the ten plagues and the fall of Jericho. Kings had once shaken at the mention of the God of Israel and his dramatic acts against those who opposed his people. Was this the same nation that now cowered under the heathen gaze of Sisera and watched as its crops were burnt, its animals stolen, its children offered as sacrifices to Canaanite gods? Even animals had more value and self-worth than we did.

By the time I rose as a mother for Israel, our villages were empty because the inhabitants had flown to neighbouring countries to escape Sisera. People did not travel on the main roads for fear of being kidnapped and used as slaves by our oppressors. Something had to be done. It was a conviction that began as a dull thud in my heart and escalated to a reverberating shout that hammered at me all the time. I knew then that the Lord was asking me if I was willing to do as he was clearly asking me. I was a prophet and a judge. Hadn't he given me particular favour with all Israel by setting me apart and giving me the title 'mother of Israel'? Despite hassles with the few men who wouldn't defer to my court judgments because of the fact that I was a woman, hadn't God for the most part protected me?

I began by talking to the people and reminding them of where their loyalties used to lie. Had they forgotten that we were a chosen nation? Had they forgotten the stories of how God delivered our ancestors from Egypt and how foreign nations cowered at the mention of the Israelite God? Was this the way we wanted to live for the rest of our lives, for ever under the sandals of Canaanites who were no better than animals? And what about God? Admittedly, we had not followed his laws, but didn't our grandmothers tell us how he always welcomed them back with open arms when they repented of turning away from him? Slowly, the people started listening to me. They started believing that change was possible.

I've noticed that God seems to put people in strategic places before using them for the real task he has in store for them. Perhaps you are one of those people. You might hold a particular position in your family, community, church or place of work, but you are not really sure what your purpose is. Or maybe, just like me, he's placed you in a unique and clearly defined role. The key is not to be afraid but to start living each day at a time and waiting for God to lead you where you are meant to go. The process of revelation—and it is a process—might take a while to unfold but if God does not appear to be in a hurry, why should you be? For instance, take my situation. I didn't become a prophet, judge or 'warrior' overnight. It was a lifetime's process and each position served to further the Lord's purpose of using me to lead the Israelites to victory over Sisera. Yes, I was a woman, but I figured that God had at various times used a burning bush, a donkey and mere men to communicate to his people, so why not a woman?

Leading a battle is not all it's cracked up to be

I had a few disappointments—like when I told Barak that the Lord had given us the victory over Sisera. All he had to do was to assemble 10,000 warriors from the tribes of Napthali and Zebulun at Mount Tabor, and the Lord would do the rest. Barak dug his heels in and insisted that he wasn't going anywhere without me along-side. I was annoyed. Firstly, women did not go to the battlefront. We stayed behind in our fortified cities, pouring down boiling water and throwing stones from the walls as our enemies tried to force their way through the city gates. Secondly, did he really think my presence would make a difference? The Lord had declared that we would win, so what did Barak need me there for? But I agreed to go with them because I realized that action was required, not my retorts. I wasn't to know that, through this, God would honour me. To this day, I am known as Deborah, the prophetess and judge who marched with the men to victory. The irony is that all I did was march with the men.

To be honest with you, there wasn't really a battle. The Lord had said that Barak simply had to get the Israelite warriors to Mount Tabor and he would do the rest. He wasn't kidding. As Barak advanced, the Lord routed Sisera and all his chariots with the sword and Barak pursued them all the way to Harosheth Haggoyim, where every single member of Sisera's army was killed—although the man himself had escaped on foot at Mount Tabor (Judges 4:15–17). The Israelites were amply aided by an outpouring of rain and hail that blinded the enemy and flooded the River Kishon, so that they were swept away. And thus, the battle was won. So you see, readers, the Israelites did not really do anything. The Lord accomplished the victory for them.

Let's go back to Sisera. As I said, he escaped at Mount Tabor and fled on foot to the tent of Jael, the wife of Heber who was on friendly relations with King Jabin. He thought he was safe because she was a woman and no one would think to look for him in a woman's tent. Weary in body, he asked her for something to drink and she gave him milk. But when he fell into an exhausted sleep, Jael crept up to him with a mallet and drove one of the tent pegs through his temple and then into the ground, just to ensure that he was truly dead. Many people have commented on the horrific way that Jael killed Sisera. Yes, it was gruesome but as we didn't have guns, grenades or rocket launchers in those days, we had to be inventive with our weapons of destruction. People forget that the tent peg was the only weapon at Jael's disposal. She was running out of time, so she did the only thing she could do and did it quickly.

'But how could she?' some of you are still asking. Well, Jael was married to Heber, a Kenite. Although Kenites had always been allies with Israel, Heber supported Jabin and in the process alienated his family from their Israelite neighbours. I don't think that Heber realized the full extent of what he was doing. Perhaps, if he had, he would have stopped to think. As it was, he made his family an island in a society where people valued relationships above all else. No wonder, then, that when Sisera escaped from the battle and went to Jael's tent, thinking he would be safe, he got the biggest shock of his life. I'll say something for Jael, though. After she killed Sisera, her husband looked at her in a different light. I think it was fear...

My march to the battlefield and Jael's actions did much for the reputation of Israelite women. Many was the time when I would hear a woman remark to her spouse, 'Remember Jael...' Even the men who had previously fought against my position as judge seemed to look at me with a new kind of respect. They took my judgments seriously after that—and as for my husband, let's just say that he was one of the proudest men who ever walked the roads of Ephraim.

6

Michal: a life of disappointments

Contrary to what everyone thinks, I wasn't always a miserable so-and-so. There was a time when I laughed and cried with joy much like every normal woman. And yet when people mention my name, all they remember is the woman who despised David because he danced like a commoner 'for the Lord' (2 Samuel 6:14, CEV). If only life were that simple! It is not often (if ever) that I get the opportunity to present my side of the story, as I'm often bypassed in favour of Bathsheba (I'll get to her later) or some other more 'deserving' woman, so I'm going to make full use of this opportunity. And I make no apologies for it.

One of the first princesses

My father Saul was a huge man, taller than anyone else in Israel and with looks that made grown men and women weep with envy. In spite of everything that has been written about him, I still maintain that he was one of the greatest kings of Israel. David might have loved God but he was a hypocrite through and through. My father was far from perfect, but everything he did was done in the open—unlike David, philanderer *par excellence* and murderer. How I hated him!

My father had five children with my mother Ahinoam: Jonathan, Jishui, Malchishua, Merab and me—Michal, the youngest. My early life was wonderful. Before Saul was anointed and crowned as the first king of Israel, I did what every young woman did: I got under everyone's feet around the house and did the chores that needed doing, all the while fantasizing about the day I would eventually be married myself. That was all that women dreamt about in those days. We knew our place and didn't fight for something else, because we understood the value of what we did as mothers and household managers. And no, most of us didn't worry about being second-best to men. We didn't have the time or, I have to admit, the inclination. Life was too short and our society too violent. Our days revolved around our men, homes and the daily business of living. Our men were always off to war so we had to order our households and farm the land. Because we didn't always know when or if our husbands would come back from war (and there was *always* a battle being fought), we lived each day as it came.

But enough of all that. You're not listening to my story to get an overview of biblical history. You want to know more about me, Michal, the most famous sourpuss of all time.

As I have said, my father was the first and, in my opinion, one of the greatest kings of Israel. I have to keep repeating that because it seems as if history would like to let his legacy die, and I am determined not to let that happen. They say that David was one of the greatest kings of Israel. Why? What did he really do? He went to war, had a lot of women, made a mess of his personal life and, under him, the kingdom of Israel threatened to split in half. For all my father's shortcomings, Israel remained as one nation while he was king. David couldn't even manage that. Fool! I loathe him and everything he has ever done to my family and myself. He destroyed my life, and those of my father and my sibling. Try as I might, I cannot let that go. The hurt and the pain I suffered at his hands have gone too deep.

When my father became the first king of Israel, everything changed. Suddenly, we were being fêted by everyone. We also had to learn a whole new way of life. Because the royal court of Israel was being set up from scratch, everything had to be laid out, tested and refined. And I mean everything: court positions, royal commands, ceremonies… you name it, it had to be established on a new basis. It wasn't too bad, actually, as we had the prophet Samuel to clarify matters when needed. This same prophet turned against my father when he needed him most, but we'll get to that later.

It was so exciting having a king. Finally, Israel could be like other nations! My father led and fought some battles and God gave him victory. That was when God was on Saul's side, but it wasn't long before he turned on him as well. Do you see a pattern here? Everyone who was supposed to support my father eventually turned on him. Saul had no one to trust, no one at all. Is it any wonder his life turned out the way it did? I admit that he had low self-esteem. He was also far too impatient and impetuous, but never in a million years did I think things would end the way they did. And, to be honest, I think God did over-react a bit when it came to our family. So my father messed up again and again—but it wasn't his fault! He was under pressure. He had to look good in front of his people all the time, and this led him to make some less-than-intelligent decisions. Since when was that a crime?

Look at David. Some people have said that I had no right to criticize him for dancing in the streets and with the people in a manner unbecoming to a king. But, listen! My father was royalty, and he taught and showed me how true royalty behaved. What did David know? He was tending sheep when my father was crowned the first king of Israel. I know all about royal dignity, and David did not bother to learn the lessons. I pointed it out to him and he put me in a harem for the rest of my days. That was fine with me, anyway. I didn't want his bloodstained hands on me.

David, David, David—the man of a thousand personalities. I don't know why I had such high expectations of him. He was from the tribe of Judah and I was from the tribe of Benjamin. Good stock, my tribe was. Maybe it was because I had stupid ideals about what David could be that everything went badly wrong. Maybe I could have changed something, somehow adjusted myself better to my ever-changing circumstances… or maybe my life was meant to be one never-ending disappointment. I guess I'll never know, but I do know this: my life did not start the way it ended. And I hear some of you saying, 'Such is life'.

I wish you'd known David the way I knew him when we were first married. He was, quite simply, a star. He was 'a mighty man of valour, a man of war, prudent in speech and a handsome person and the Lord was with him' (1 Samuel 16:18, NASB). And he could strum a harp unlike anyone I'd ever heard! It seemed as if there was nothing he couldn't do. Every man wanted to be his friend, and every woman his wife—including me. David used to come to the house to play the harp for Saul every time he was 'ill'—temporarily insane. I made sure I lurked nearby when he was there. Not that I was the only one. In fact, now I come to think about it, all the women of the household found excuses to hang around when he was visiting. I could go one better than the other women, though. I was a princess and my brother, Jonathan, was also David's best friend.

Some people have accused me of lacking in character. They say I only fell for David because of his good looks and because he was the action man of his day. He killed Goliath, played the harp and had looks to die for. He was also single and available. Well, I defy anyone not to fall for such a man! Was my love for him any different from your celebrity worship on earth today? I was a young girl, still in my teens, a budding flower, and David was my prince. I loved him. I thought he loved me. Why else would he go to all the trouble of getting 200 Philistine foreskins for my dowry when my father only asked for a hundred? What bravery, and how it turned my head! Getting the foreskin of a Philistine, one of our most ferocious and barbaric enemies, was considered a feat, but to get 200 was a sign of supernatural courage. I was in love! David and I were going to do great things together. If only I'd known how my foolish dreams would turn to ashes in the cold light of day!

My father Saul was battling against the goads, I know that now. He was battling with himself and with God, even if he didn't realize it at the time. He also underestimated just how seriously God viewed obedience. End result: a lifetime of ceaseless strife and bouts of insanity. Even so, I think the Lord was too harsh on my father. Saul wasn't perfect, but neither was David, the usurper that the

Lord put on the throne to replace my father. When Saul realized that his children would not inherit his throne and that God had, in fact, given the throne to David, he simply lost his mind. All parents want to leave a legacy of some sort to their children. For my father, that legacy was his throne, and the knowledge that he couldn't pass it on was more than he could bear.

Even worse was knowing that Jonathan, his heir to the throne, continuously conspired against him to ensure that David would be the next king of Israel. Such acts of betrayal, for a parent, are very hard to digest. Jonathan and my father used to argue all the time. Saul was aware that his control of the kingdom was slipping away and he was frantically trying to hang on to it, any way he could. He was a desperate man and he did desperate things. I just wish that people would get over this and look at the situation from his perspective. How would they feel if they knew that something they had built from scratch was being taken from them and given to someone deemed 'more worthy'? Wouldn't they stay and fight with every weapon they had? If, for you, the answer to this is 'yes', then how can you condemn my father? And to those of you shaking your heads and thinking, 'Well, God had given the throne to David and Saul should have accepted it', all I have to say is, 'Bah! Humbug! Try being in my father's shoes for a single minute and we'll see if you're still shaking that tambourine.'

I talked earlier about the kind of life we women lived in those days. In many ways, we were at the mercy of the men who ruled our lives. Occasionally, we would be blessed with good, kind husbands who looked upon us not as possessions but as human beings with value. I once knew somebody like that. His name was Palti. He showed me what true love meant. He was a Benjaminite, the same as me. He was also decent, loving and kind—unlike the barbaric men from the tribe of Judah. This is what happened: after our wedding, David had to go on the run to escape from my father, who was trying to kill him. He ended up in Philistine territory. My father wanted to spite him, so he gave me away to another man, Palti.

When Saul killed himself in battle, my half-brother Ishbosheth became the king of Israel. When he accused Abner, the commander of the army, of sleeping with Rizpah, my father's concubine, Abner changed allegiance and went over to David. The significance of this is clear, even today. It is no secret in government that whoever is in charge of the army has control of the country. That is why unstable leaders of equally unstable countries either strengthen the army to solidify their hold on the country, or weaken it so as to render it ineffective.

David was a strategist. When Abner came to him, he told Abner he would not negotiate with him until I, his wife, was returned to him. And that was what happened—end of story. I wasn't so stupid as to think David wanted me because he missed me. I was a possession that had been taken from him and he wanted me back. Second, and most importantly, I was a visible means of uniting all the tribes. I was the daughter of the previous king, who had tried to kill him, and by bringing me back to his house David was showing how 'forgiving' he was. In addition, Ishbosheth, the present king, wasn't exactly doing well, so who better to unite all these factors and consolidate David's claim to the throne than me?

The downward spiral

David had been on the run for many, many years. He had also collected more wives, concubines and children along the way. He could have easily left me with Palti. Palti wasn't hurting anybody. Our life was simple; we weren't looking for trouble. Fine, David was my legal husband but he'd been gone a long time. To all intents and purposes, Palti was my husband, not David. But my life wasn't mine to live or to choose. It was the men who dictated the way my life would go. So off to David I went, followed by Palti, who bawled his heart out for the whole journey. If there was anyone I wished had been spared all this heartache, it would have been him. He was a pawn in the game between my father, David and all the other useless men that summed up my life.

How to describe my feelings? One day I was married to David and the next 'married' to Palti. Then I was 'given' back to David. I had no voice and no one to fight for me. My dear Palti did not take it well at all. In all the centuries since then, has anyone sought to consider his feelings? No, it's better to focus on Michal, the bitter one, who despised David. Give a woman a break...

I wish with all my heart that David had married Merab, my older sister, when he was given the opportunity. Saul did offer her to him but David insisted that it was me he wanted to marry. If he had married Merab, it would have saved me all this emotional pain, but such is life. Sometimes we don't have much control over what happens. We just do the best we can with the blows life deals us, and yes, I was handed a lot of blows. David did damage to my sister as well. He rounded up her five sons and had them executed when the Gibeonites said that Saul was responsible for massacring their people. It seems that God had a hand in this as well. Apparently he said that there was a famine in the land because the blood of the Gibeonites was on my father and, by default, on my nephews' heads: an eye for an eye and a tooth for a tooth. Merab spent seven months by the grave of her sons. She went almost crazy with grief. And there I was, imprisoned in the harem, unable to comfort her.

This marriage business—it has caused wars and ruined a lot of lives. If I had the means, I would caution every woman not to go into it. Far better to live a life alone than face a lifetime of pure strife. I had 14 years of happiness with Palti and then, just like that, I was brought back to David as a possession. No one thought once about me, what I wanted and what my needs were. Even worse, I knew David had no use for me. I was just one of the many women he had dotted all over the palace and harem. I hated him being around me and touching me. Because of him, I lost the only man who ever truly loved me, my brothers were dead, my father was dead, and my nephews were murdered. Perhaps it was a blessing in disguise that I never had children, although enough people have said that I was cursed with barrenness. If you were in my position, would you want to bring children into the world and have them endure the kind of life I lived? Of course not.

Dear reader, you were probably so quick to judge me before. Well, now that you've heard my story, how do you feel towards me? It seems to me that I was the one making all the sacrifices, suffering for the incompetence of the men around me, and when I dared to chastise my 'husband' for behaving with such indignity in front of his people, I was labelled a shrew.

I don't even know why, over the centuries, I have been judged for such a small incident. You didn't see David, dressed like a priest and flailing his body in a terrible attempt at dancing, all in full sight of his people. Was this the way a king ought to behave? Seeing him brought back bitter memories of my father, my brothers and Palti, and how, because of David, they were forced out of my life for ever. And here was David, dancing before his God and rejoicing in the middle of my pain. How could he? So I told him exactly what I thought of him when he came to the palace: that he did the royal family an indignity by dancing on the streets without any decorum, simply because the ark was in the city. He replied by telling me that God had chosen him over my family to rule Israel, and if I had issues with that fact, it was my problem, not his. He said other things that I will not repeat here. Suffice it to say, our relationship became distinctly icy after that.

Remember, my father was the first king of Israel. He wasn't perfect, but he still held his head high. He learned all about royalty. He created it and lived it, most of the time with dignity. Who was David? A shepherd boy with delusions of grandeur. During the ten or so years he was on the run from my father, he was no more than a vagabond, a marauding raider and, even worse, a murderer with a wandering eye. He married women at will and kept even more in stock as concubines. His son Solomon might have had the reputation of the 'wisest man alive' but he was just plain stupid when he came to women. Scripture distinctly recalls him as having 300 wives and 700 concubines. I guess stupidity was ingrained in his family...

Call me what you want, but at least admit that life did not deal with me fairly. As a woman, I did not expect my life to be easy, but I do expect a certain leniency from the judgment of history because of my hardships. I would have loved to have a child with my beloved Palti; I rejoice for those times when I was with him. And despite the injustice of being shovelled from one man to another, the alternative was to be alone and loved by nobody, while my supposed husband finished his mercenary activities. My memories of Palti sustained me during those lonely years in the harem.

My dearly beloved Palti, I miss him terribly. We were not married in the formal sense of the word, but in my heart of hearts he was and still remains my husband—not David, the king of Israel, who never truly loved me.

The Bathsheba saga

No, David's relationship with Bathsheba didn't surprise me. As I have said, he was always stupid when he came to women. What did surprise me was the lengths he went to in order to cover his crime. But this time, God showed David that he wasn't immune from wrath, and that pleased me, enormously. Justice was served at last! I was beginning to think it was a fantasy reserved only for the foolish. And as for Bathsheba, the answer is no, I never envied her. The way I felt, she was welcome to David and the trouble that usually followed the women associated with him. There were times when I felt sorry for her, though. It wasn't her fault that she slept with David and fell pregnant with his child, even though she was still married to someone else. David was the king. He saw her, wanted her and made sure he had her. It wasn't in her power to refuse. He hadn't bargained with the risk that she would get pregnant. Fearful of the scandal that would break, he arranged to have her husband killed and then brought her to the palace.

I wonder how Bathsheba kept her head during those times. The servants were muttering, while the other wives and concubines were shooting dark looks at her and saying that she probably wanted her husband dead so she could be a 'queen'. I suppose I didn't make her life any easier, either. I simply ignored her. I had too much of my own turmoil to deal with. But even so, my heart went out to her when she lost her baby. That was tragic and, contrary to what everyone thinks, losing a baby is something I would never wish on any woman. I am a woman myself, childless but still a woman. I could go on about the whole Bathsheba business but I think she should tell her story herself. It's right after mine, in the next chapter, so you don't have long to wait.

Being disappointed, not bitter

Having said all this, there are quite a few things I wish I'd done differently. In hindsight, I think I should have stopped railing against my circumstances and letting anger consume me. Anger is a tiresome business. I think I should have tried to get comfort else-where. Jonathan always had a great relationship with the God of Israel, but I didn't. When I was a child, he was someone to whom we made sacrifices and whom we called upon when we needed help with things like winning battles and so on. And later, he was just someone who sat back and allowed my life to be manipulated by the men who were supposed to protect me. Many times, I would call to whoever was out there and ask for deliverance from all that was happening to me, but no help ever seemed to come. Maybe, instead of deliverance, I should have asked for wisdom to help me cope with what was going on.

Take the Palti situation. When I was returned to David, I probably should have tried to think of myself as his wife again. Yes, the circumstances were far from ideal, but clinging to those memories of Palti probably did not help. How could I live in the present when I was stuck in memories of the past? It was the same with my constant comparisons of David and my father. The truth, however bitter, was that Saul did not come up to scratch. He relied too much on the praise of men and not enough on the Lord. His sense of inferiority dogged him until the day he died. He wasn't really fit to lead Israel and, if we were to be the nation God had called us to be, we needed a leader with God's own heartbeat to take us there. That person was David. I knew this, deep down, but did not want to confront it. It felt easier to blame him.

My father... Jonathan... Abner... David... these men had the power of life and death over me and they chose to play with me as if I were of no consequence. I should have dealt with my pain, anger, hurt and bitterness over this, but I didn't. It was easier to nurture my negative feelings because they gave me strength to rise above my circumstances. I didn't know that the bitterness was slowly killing me inside, robbing me of my ability to see clearly and, most importantly, accept God's help. If I had cried out to God in my pain, for wisdom and help, he would have shown me that although David's heart was to do God's will all the time, his humanity got in the way a lot of the time. God would have made me see how fortunate I was to have a brother who loved the Lord so much that he didn't mind God choosing someone else to lead Israel, even though he, Jonathan, was the heir to the throne. God would have shown me these men as he saw them. He would have reminded me that despite all their imperfections, he loved them and was using them to fulfil his purpose for Israel and, ultimately, the whole world. But because I didn't allow God near me, I wasn't able to see all that. More's the shame. I would have saved myself a lifetime of loneliness and despair. Who knows, maybe David would even have divorced me and let me go back to Palti? Well, maybe not, but a woman is allowed to dream, isn't she?

Letting go, being free

It takes more energy to be angry than it does to be free. Like every other woman in this book, I learned that letting go of pain and anger does not happen overnight, but it can happen. The God of Israel is a God of miracles and second chances. He can change a situation in the blink of an eye, or wait until our characters are formed in the midst of the challenging situation before doing something about it. Look at Leah, she of 'married single' fame. Her life certainly did not change overnight. It took the loss of her sister for her to see all that the Lord had been trying to teach her about relying on him for grace and strength amid seemingly insurmountable difficulties. One day she woke up and realized that obedience to God was more important than anything else. How I wish I had had her wisdom when I was still on earth!

You've read my story. You've heard my pain, and you may have rejoiced because you have found someone who shares your life experiences, but don't leave it there. Allow me to set you on the way to true peace by daring you to let go of your pain, anger and bitterness. Life has probably dealt you some hard knocks; or perhaps your life has been dictated by external forces very much outside your control, and by people who were supposed to take care of you. I understand. I had my choices taken from me too. But I had a glimpse of heaven when I was with Palti, just as you must have had glimpses of heaven at one point or another. Hold on to those glimpses, and then ask the Lord to enable you to let go of the past and look forward to the future. The hardest step is always the first one. If you need help doing it, pray—even if you have to do it through gritted teeth.

As for me, I'm still learning and trying to make sense of it all.

7

Bathsheba: it wasn't the sex

Don't worry. You didn't buy the wrong book, and I'm definitely not about to go into details of my sex life with David, the man after God's own heart—the man who killed my husband to cover up his affair with me. He's also goes by another name: one of the greatest kings of Israel.

I have to admit it, I simply don't get God. Just when I think I have him all figured out, he goes and pulls the rug from under my feet and I am left with the remnants of my assumptions about him. I really thought David and the Lord had something going. I always thought that David had some kind of insight into the Lord's heart. Never did I imagine that God would punish David for killing Uriah by allowing my son—my son!—to die. When my child died from an illness allowed by God, I realized that God doesn't have favourites and that we are all still subject to his laws and responsible for keeping them. There is a reason why he gave us those laws, and when we break them we have to face the consequences. Believe me when I say how devastating those consequences can be.

I assume you've read Michal's story, so you know of me or about me. Poor Michal. She was dealt some hard knocks, wasn't she? For what it's worth, David didn't have an easy life either, and neither did I. It's one thing to have an affair and kill someone to cover it up, but it's another thing entirely to have your family turn into some sort of freak show as a consequence of your actions. And David certainly suffered, in a major way. Leah was wrong. *I* should be the one on a TV chat show.

I'm going to tell you my story, and I would like you to listen and even take some notes. Most importantly, I would like you not to pass judgment either on me or on David. He loved the Lord. He was a great leader—indeed, one of the greatest ever—but he knew nothing about being a father or a husband, much less how to lead a family. He was a great military strategist and warrior, but all that counted for nothing because he didn't have the skills to lead the most important group of all—his family. It proved to be his undoing. It also led to one of the most turbulent times in Israel's history.

How not to sleep with the king

David was a valiant man with a profound weakness for women. I guess he couldn't help himself, or maybe it was the society we lived in that made him thus. You've heard Leah's and Michal's stories. Back in those days, our men literally had the power of life and death over us. Once in a while, the Lord raised up great women like Deborah to lead the nation, but on the whole we were at the complete mercy of these men—or so it seemed. Little did they know that we fought our battles in prayer and in the hearts of the children we raised.

Like I said, many of our men seemed to have a great weakness for women, as if they weren't able to control themselves. I sometimes wonder what our society would have been like if the women had suddenly started bedding the men with the same blatant disregard for their feelings—whether it would have caused the same degree of heartache that the men wreaked upon our lives. I doubt it.

My story begins with a day that started like any other. I woke up, did my household tasks, went about the business of living. My husband Uriah wasn't around as he was on the battlefront, fighting the Ammonites. Incidentally, he was one of the famous Band of Thirty, a group of fighters that King David personally chose as part of his inner core of bodyguards, so he was well known to the king. Apart from my usual undercurrent of fear, wondering if I would be made a widow before sundown, there was no reason to think that the day would end differently from the one before. I'd finished my period and had just done the purification rites when I got the summons from the king.

Initially, I didn't know what to expect. I'd assumed that, being the king, he would have been on the battlefront with the rest of his men. But before very long, I think I knew what he wanted. He was a king and his love of women was well known. Even so, I assumed I was protected by virtue of the fact that I was married. Then again, the men were at war, so that gave David leeway to do whatever he wanted with me. I won't go into the details but here's what happened: I was summoned to come to the palace. I obeyed. The king declared undying lust for me and we slept together. Afterwards, I went home. Not long after that, I found out I was pregnant.

I've thought a lot about that day. Sometimes I think I didn't try hard enough not to sleep with David, but exactly what could I have done? He was the king of Israel, and not just any king. He was King David, who slew Goliath when he was little more than a boy. He was a strong man, valiant, and very virile. In terms of physical strength, he won hands down. How could I have fought him off me? I did the only thing I felt I could do in those circumstances: I gave in to him because it made everything easier.

At other times, when I think back, I wonder whether I was flattered by his attention. A king, lusting after me? Unbelievable! And not just anyone but King David! Most of the time, though, I just wish the whole sorry business had never taken place. Whether he was a king or not, I was a married woman whose husband was out defending our nation from marauding raiders while I was committing adultery. I felt so dirty when we had finished and I was sent home. I held my head low, because I couldn't bear to see the servants' knowing looks when I passed them. I didn't want anyone to remember seeing me there. That sexual act between David and me was for one time only, I thought. I hadn't counted on getting pregnant and the drastic steps that David would take to protect himself.

You see, this is the illusion born of moral failure, or compromise, or whatever discreet word you call it on earth nowadays. I prefer to call it by its original name: sin. It's a disease that, if left unchecked, can suck the life out of someone's soul. Although I had had no choice in sleeping with David, it had certainly happened and we had to face the consequences. The moment I realized I was pregnant, I did the only reasonable thing a woman in my position could do: I sent a message to the king. David knew the child was his. My husband was still at the battlefront and had been for some time, so everyone would know that he wasn't the father. Besides, I had already made up my mind that I wasn't going to be humiliated in the eyes of the whole community on my own. David and I were in this situation together and we were going to face the consequences together. I thought I didn't even care what David did. I just wanted him to solve the problems, and he did—or at least he tried to.

He sent word to the battlefront for Uriah to be brought to him, and then tried to get my husband to come home and sleep with me. David was clever but he didn't know my husband. Uriah was a man of great integrity. Twice David gave him royal permission to go home to me and enjoy a break from the battlefield, and twice he refused on the basis that he couldn't go home and make merry with his wife when his comrades were fighting a war. When David got fed up of arguing, he told his commander-in-chief, Joab, to place Uriah in the middle of the fiercest fighting so that he was likely to be killed—and that's exactly what happened.

I mourned him. I truly did, because, contrary to what everyone thinks, I didn't want him to die. It wasn't his fault that he got caught in the crossfire of David's madness. I mourned in the midst of my shame as my pregnant belly started to show. By now, people were talking. There were whispers that David was the father of my child, although no one said anything outright to me. As soon as the required mourning period was over, David sent for me. I became one of his wives, for my own protection. If he hadn't taken me in, I would have been an outcast. I would have had to deal alone with the shame I'd heaped on my family and husband's family. Marrying me and putting me in the palace was the best thing that David could have done for me. Finally, I thought, I can leave the past and look to the future. I wasn't to know that catastrophe was round the corner.

Just remember: there is always a cost

Yes, flattery certainly is a powerful thing. I liken my first visit to the palace for sex with David to the fixation some women have with celebrities. There you are in a concert, having the time of your life. You're not sure, but you could almost believe that the rapper, musician or whoever is flailing about on the stage has got his eye on you. Wait! You're not mistaken. He does have his eye on you! He makes a quick signal for you to come backstage after the concert. Hesitantly, you make your way there. You're not sure what to expect, but what have you got to lose? He chose you out of the hundreds and thousands of women in that stadium. And suddenly, there he is in the flesh. The two of you hurriedly get down to it. It's over, and before you know it, you're being bustled out and down the corridor by one of his handlers. Wait! Isn't this the same guy who smiled at you when you first came backstage not too long ago? Well, the guy who smiled now wants you out of the way. You've fulfilled your purpose for the night. You're ashamed, but defiant. What do you care? You slept with a celebrity!

Does that sound familiar to anyone out there? You're married but you're having a secret relationship with another person. You know what you're doing but you feel you can't help yourself. Your new partner really 'understands' you. In fact, you've convinced yourself that your extra-marital affair is actually helping your marriage on the road to recovery. Rubbish! You can dress it up any way you like, but in your heart of hearts you surely know that what you're doing is wrong. You're no different from David. He had multiple wives, concubines and many children. He knew that God frowned upon polygamy but I guess he felt that he couldn't help himself. His lack of control caused him and others no end of trouble.

I talked earlier about sin. It affects us on so many levels—emotional, spiritual and, in some cases, physical. Not too long after David got me settled in the palace, we had a visit from the prophet Nathan, and this is the message he brought for David, straight from the mouth of God himself: 'Why, then, have you despised the word of the Lord and done this horrible deed? For you have murdered Uriah and stolen his wife. From this time on, the sword will be a constant threat in your family, because you have despised me by taking Uriah's wife to be your own. Because of what you have done, I, the Lord, will cause your own household to rebel against you. I will give your wives to another man, and he will go to bed with them in public view. You did it secretly, but I will do this to you openly in the sight of all Israel' (2 Samuel 12:9–12, NLT).

Ouch. After reading this, could anyone still feel the same way about an extra-marital affair? They might not have killed anyone but God's law against adultery still stands. He views the marriage vows very seriously. You may feel as if your marriage is on its last legs. Either or both partners may have suffered greatly, but an affair does not make it right. It does not satisfy the soul the way God can. Instead of looking outward for the fulfilment that may be lacking in your marriage, I have another suggestion: try looking towards God. And try your local church. They may be able to help you on the road to restoration.

Living with the consequences

Scholars and preachers probably make much of the fact that David 'loved' me. I'm sure that, in his own way, he did. Men are such complex creatures, yet, at the same time, so simple. I have never figured out how a man can profess undying love for one woman, yet insist on having other wives and concubines. 'But you're my number one,' David used to say. Of course I was. It wasn't his fault. It was the environment in which we lived in those days. I loved David and respected him greatly, but after Nathan's pronouncement on our child, I died inside. I begged and pleaded with David and with God to do something, anything, to spare my son, but I knew I was fighting a losing battle. I knew the Lord would take my child home to himself.

David refused to give up hope, though. The first night our son fell deathly ill, straight after Nathan had left, David lay down on the bare floor. He fasted for seven days, pleading with God to have mercy on his child. I veered between pleadings, anger and acceptance of the Lord's punishment. I cried out to him to take me instead and leave my child alone—but to no avail. God wasn't listening. He was making the point that innocent people are the ones most likely to suffer for somebody else's wrong actions. I could see that, but why my child? I never did understand—not that understanding would have made any difference. My son was gone.

In due course, I had other children, but I never forgot my firstborn, the son the Lord took away. All the answers in the world would not have erased the inconsolable, cold fact of his death.

I'll tell you something about David's children. They were like their father, in that they were led by their passions. Of all the things I witnessed in that palace and in my forays into the harem, none shocked me more than what I am about to tell you.

David had 19 sons, of whom four were mine. The rest were produced by his other wives and concubines. Although the children were related to each other by virtue of having the same father, they tended to live separate lives in the palace, so maybe that was how the unthinkable happened. Amnon, son of David and Ahinoam, decided that he was madly in love with his half-sister Tamar, and raped her. When I heard about it, I couldn't say or do anything, but I remembered how I was summoned to the palace at David's command, all those years before.

The scripture warns us that whatever is hidden will be brought to light. When David found out what had happened to his daughter, he was livid, but he didn't do anything about it. Maybe he thought back to when he ordered Uriah to be killed in battle. Maybe he thought that by pushing it to the back of his mind, he wouldn't ever have to deal with it. Maybe he didn't want to mete out God's required judgment for such a grievous sin, especially as it involved his own children. On the surface, it seemed that Amnon had got away with his terrible act, but Absalom, Tamar's brother, never forgot. He spent the next two years plotting Amnon's death.

Absalom couldn't forget because Tamar was living a desolate existence in his house, away from prying eyes and acid tongues. Imagine Tamar's shame, to be defiled by her own brother! She had no marriage proposals, no forays into society. In the end, Absalom had Amnon killed at a harvest feast right in front of his other brothers. He was making the point that Amnon had disgraced his sister publicly and so he had to die publicly. Afterwards, he fled to his grandfather, the king of Geshur, and stayed with him for three years. Then he was summoned back to Jerusalem by David and allowed to live there on the condition that he and David never saw each other. They managed to keep up this separation for two years.

For such a successful military strategist, David could be obtuse when it came to family matters. He never once punished Absalom for killing Amnon. Maybe, if he had used an ounce of discipline on his children, the ensuing chaos would never have happened. He thought that by ignoring problems he could make them go away, but they didn't. They just grew into bigger and bigger issues until they finally exploded.

It took Absalom a while, but when he came back from Geshur he succeeded in turning the nation against his father. They'd been reconciled with each other and David actually thought their relationship was fine. I knew better. I was a woman, and even if men know nothing else about us, they will acknowledge that we can have remarkable insight into people's hearts. It was indeed a sad day in Israel when David had to flee the country because Absalom had orchestrated an armed rebellion against him. How he wept as he went up to the Mount of Olives!

You see what I mean when I talk about facing the consequences of our actions? My husband's multiple wives, myself included, gave him many children who, in later years, would cause him much sorrow and shame. His adulterous liaison with me and the subsequent murder of my husband led to the death of our child. How much worse could it get? In fact, as time passed, it got a lot worse.

The day David left the palace, the whole of Israel lined up and watched a weeping king abdicate his throne for his son. It was a sorry sight. Was this the same man who had slain Goliath? The one who made the enemies of Israel quake in fear on hearing his name? Was this the one whom God called a man after his own heart? I held my sons close to me and prayed that the Lord would protect them. But Absalom was not done yet. He had one final act of contempt for his father. He summoned ten of David's concubines and slept with each one of them in a tent on the palace roof, in full view of everyone. For someone so beautiful, he was filled with incredible hatred. He was later killed by Joab.

A divided nation

We lived in uncertain times, confronted by death at every turn. Justice was served swiftly, and usually with the sword. It was not uncommon for whole families and communities to be wiped out in retribution for an act against a member of the attacker's family. We were constantly on edge.

In the palace, I was always on the lookout for my enemies. It was a place of intrigue, machinations and alliances. I kept my allies close to me and my enemies even closer. I changed food tasters on a regular basis and watched over my children with eagle eyes. I might have been David's beloved wife, but that didn't mean I was free from danger. If anything, it increased the threat to my life and my sons' lives. I enjoined them to keep their eyes focused on the Lord and not to deviate from the right path, but they did not listen. They were unfortunately aided in their disobedience by their father, who never punished or chastised them when they did wrong. The Bible says that if we train our children in the way they should go, they will not depart from it. I tried to do the best I could but I was on my own. I was living in a divided house with warring factions and my husband was leading a nation of warring tribes. It was a constant juggling act, requiring the patience of Job and the wisdom of God to get it right.

David was eventually reinstated as the king of Israel but I knew that he could be deposed again if one of his sons or anyone close to him rose up against him. If they succeeded, it would mean immediate death for myself and my children. The only way to secure my place was to neutralize the threat from its very roots. I was one of the king's wives. I also had sons, so I had to be clever about protecting my future and my children's future. The most effective way to do that was to plan for life beyond David's reign.

My son Solomon, the wisest man who ever lived

Solomon was a prince among men. Every mother thinks all her children are special, but there may still be a particular child who makes your heart sing by sheer virtue of who they are. In my case, that child was Solomon. He was born after the Lord took my first son away. Perhaps it was because the Lord showed him special favour that Solomon was who he was. It is no coincidence that when Adonijah decided to wrestle the throne away from David, he called all his other brothers to support him but not Solomon. Adonijah knew that there was no way Solomon would support him in such an endeavour.

When I heard that Adonijah was in the process of gathering key people to support his claim to the throne, I went straight to the king. David had already said that Solomon would rule after him, but if I didn't act, I knew it would never happen. Thank God for the prophet Nathan—the same one who brought us God's judgment regarding my first son—who helped me open David's eyes to what was going on. David had aged, but he still had full command of his faculties. Glory be to God that he realized what was happening and quickly had Solomon installed on the throne.

I have no regrets over what I did. The Lord himself had declared that my son would be king. I was merely acting on what I knew would be true. The fact of the matter, though, was that after David and I had committed that one act of adultery, I faced a lifetime of constant juggling, politicking and threats, real and imagined, to my life and the lives of my children.

Redemption

I've made much of the fact that David's sin of adultery had far-reaching consequences, which he himself never foresaw. When he summoned me to the palace, he was thinking of instant gratification. Well, he certainly got that, but I doubt he ever realized he would suffer so much as a result. On the surface, it might seem that things eventually worked out, but it's an experience I wouldn't wish on anyone.

My husband ruled Israel for 40 years, and in those years he survived numerous attempts on his life by his own sons. Michal was palmed off on to someone else and his son was killed by his commander-in-chief—though not before he had endured the humiliation of seeing this same son sleeping with his concubines in full view of all Israel. But despite everything, his faith in the Lord never wavered. God gave us a silver lining to all these sorrows and humiliation, although we didn't know this in our lifetime. He says that weeping may endure for the night but joy comes in the morning (Psalm 30:5), and David and I had our joy: our life together and the Messiah who came from our bloodline.

What message shall I leave with you? That the Lord's arms are not so short that he cannot pull you out of the pit. No matter what you're facing now—moving house, an unplanned pregnancy, or even threats to your life—believe me when I tell you that the Lord knows. He knows and cares about your situation, even if it is a consequence of your sin or someone else's sin. Turn to the Lord and let him rescue you. He rescued me and each of my sisters whose stories you hear in this book, and he can and will rescue you too. All you have to do is ask.

8

Esther: beauty pageants, genocide and festivals

I was raised by Mordecai, my cousin, a minor official at the court of King Xerxes. Many people focus on the fact that God used me to prevent a possible genocide of the Jewish nation, but I prefer to emphasize the relationship I had with my cousin. I honoured and respected him and always acted on his advice because I knew he had nothing but the best in mind for me. If the Lord had not placed him in the palace at the time when I was there, I don't know what would have happened to me and my people.

King Xerxes was a very impetuous man and given to excess. Nothing he did was on a small scale. He ruled over many lands, stretching from Ethiopia to India. If he built a palace, it had to be grand and mind-blowingly ostentatious. If he gave a banquet, it had to be big, flamboyant and, above all, majestic, simply because he had to prove that he had the power and the wealth to make it so. Xerxes denied himself nothing. He was worshipped as a god by his people.

One day, during one of his banquets, drunk on wine and full of pride, he summoned the queen to appear before his guests so that he could show off her beauty. But she refused to come. Xerxes was outraged. How dare she? Didn't she know that he had the power of life and death over her? Quickly, he summoned his advisers and sought their counsel as to how he could punish her. The advisers thought long and hard and finally one of them, Memucan, came up with an answer. He thought that all the noblewomen who heard about the queen's behaviour would doubtless use it as an excuse to be disrespectful to their own husbands, causing discord throughout the land. So he advised the king to issue a decree, banishing Queen Vashti from his presence, and to give the queen's title to someone else.

Xerxes did not waste any time. He sent messengers to all parts of the kingdom, proclaiming that every man should be the ruler of his own home. Throughout this time, I was living with my cousin Mordecai, whom I also called father. Royal matters were not of much concern to me, as they were too far removed from my life, and I wasn't married anyway, so I didn't pay much attention to this proclamation. Mordecai didn't encourage idle chatter, so I couldn't talk about it with him. All in all, life went on as usual.

Later Xerxes told me he wasn't happy. He started thinking about Vashti. No, he hadn't done the right thing by listening to Memucan and issuing that edict banishing her from his presence for ever. He missed her and he wanted her back, but how? His proclamation had gone out into all the kingdoms, and couldn't be repealed—his advisers made sure of that. So what could he do in the meantime? His eyes narrowed as he thought of his advisers' eagerness to get rid of his queen...

Xerxes was right to suspect his advisers. With a kingdom stretching across three continents, intrigue and political manoeuvring were the order of the day. He couldn't possibly know what was happening in every nook and cranny of his lands so he had to rely on his advisers to inform him. The advisers, in turn, made alliances and betrayed each other at will. In the end, they got rid of a queen who wasn't furthering their own personal ambitions.

The king was growing agitated. He could decide to accuse his advisers of poisoning his mind against his queen and have them executed as traitors. At this point the advisers were fortunate enough to come up with a solution. They approached the king cautiously: 'Let a search be made for beautiful young virgins for the king. Let the king appoint commissioners in every province of his realm to bring all these beautiful girls into the harem at the citadel of Susa. Let them be placed under the care of Hegai, the king's eunuch, who is in charge of the women; and let beauty treatments be given to them. Then let the girl who pleases the king be queen instead of Vashti' (Esther 2:2–4). Xerxes loved the idea. All those women, just for him!

It concerns everybody

When the messengers declared the royal edict, Mordecai and I, once again, did not take much notice. We paid little attention to events outside of home because they didn't concern us. I am sure you are the same. Maybe you have no interest in current affairs, you do not watch the news or read the newspapers, because you believe that the events being reported have no relevance to you. You're too busy to listen, and besides, who wants to be exposed to the depressing information that they spew out continuously?

Mordecai and I thought as you did: we heard the news, did nothing about it, and went on with our lives, because we naturally assumed that it applied to other people, not us—until the day they came for me, a young girl, to take me to the harem. Suddenly it wasn't somebody else. *I* was the news, the story. Next time you hear the news, don't turn off the television or radio and go back to leading your own life! One day, you might be the news item, and then you will wonder why no one else is paying attention. There are so many events happening on earth that are warning signs of what is yet to unfold, but these signs are being ignored because no one is taking notice. Remember the words of the Bible exhorting us to pray for our governments.

Everyone knew what happened when a young woman was taken away to the harem. She would spend one night with the king in the palace and then be banished for ever to the harem, never to see her family again. If her first night with the king was memorable, she might spend a few more nights with him, but usually the king simply accumulated more and more young women and discarded them to the harem once he was finished with them. The only men allowed near these women were eunuchs. It was no wonder that many of the women almost went mad with loneliness and boredom. They were not allowed out of the harem except when summoned to the king. As the king's concubines, they were not free to marry, yet they were forgotten after their one night of passion was over. Their only option was to ensure that they had children to consolidate their claim on the king, and the women employed every weapon at their disposal to increase their chances: even poisoning their fellow concubines, or accusing each other of having intimate relationships with the palace guards—an act of treason punishable only by death. Of course, friendships were also made in the harem, but they were very guarded relationships. For the most part, the women viewed each other as adversaries in the fight to gain the attentions of the king.

At the time, I didn't know all this but Mordecai did. The look on his face when the messengers came for me broke my heart. A man not given to affection, he drew me close and told me what an honour it was for me to be chosen as one of the young women to be presented to the king. He said that I need not fear because he would ask after me every day, and everything was going to be fine. I believed him, because he had never lied to me. His whole life had been devoted to observing the Law and raising me to be a virtuous Jewish girl, and he had succeeded. I can say that because everyone commended him on what a fine job he had done with me, his cousin, who was 'lovely in form and features' (Esther 2:7). The one thing he forbade me to do was to tell anyone about my Jewish background. I obeyed him because I trusted him. He had never once given me a reason not to do so.

I am often asked how it was that I gained the favour of Hegai, one of the eunuchs. My reply is that I didn't do anything. I did as I was told, I didn't involve myself in harem politics and I meditated on God's laws constantly—in secret, though. When God seemed far away, it made me feel better to know that Mordecai was nearby, praying for me. A combination of all these factors meant that I pleased Hegai immensely, and he was the eunuch in charge of the 'pageant girls'. In fact, Hegai was so pleased with me that he gave me special food, selected seven maids from the king's palace for me and moved me to the best place in the harem, away from prying eyes. I didn't know then that the Lord was keeping me safe from those who might have plotted to kill me because I was getting so much attention from Hegai, who controlled the women's access to the king.

Down the centuries, some people have commented that my night of passion with the king was no different from prostitution. But by the same token, I have been esteemed for allowing God to use me to deliver my people from possible extinction. In my defence, I would say that it was in neither my nor Mordecai's power to refuse the king. The truth of the matter was that young girls were regularly taken from their homes, streets and market places to satisfy the king's lust. He had spies all over the provinces, specially trained to seek out young virgins for him. It would also come as a surprise to some people today to know that many families encouraged their daughters to hang around the palace in the hope of catching the king's eye. They saw it as a chance to escape their humdrum and poverty-stricken lives. Who knows, maybe the king would execute his queen on a whim and put their daughter in the queen's place! Foolish thoughts, but no more different from those harboured by people on earth in the present day, intent on seducing famous married celebrities so that they too can be in the public eye.

Our preparation to be presented to the king took a year. In that year, I learned about beauty treatments and the art of pleasing a king. Hegai did not spare me any details, and I spared my cousin *all* the details. It came to pass that when I was summoned to the king, he was attracted to me more than to any of the other women, and I won his favour and approval.

What a relief! Xerxes made me queen and Mordecai offered up a prayer of thankfulness. God had proved himself on my behalf. I was not to be banished to the harem for ever. I was a married woman. My virtue was protected. Mordecai could breathe more easily, and so could I. I was young, though, and I had yet to learn that life has a way of springing challenges when we least expect them…

Haman the horrible

Haman was a terror, no doubt about it. King Xerxes had promoted him to the rank of prime minister and he milked his position for all it was worth. Under Xerxes' command, every royal official at the king's gate had to kneel down and pay honour to Haman. But one person refused—Mordecai. Haman was a mere man, he reasoned, so why should he accord him the honour that was due only to God? Later, Haman discovered that Mordecai was a Jew, one of the people that he hated beyond reason, and he decided that he would find a way to destroy them throughout Xerxes' kingdom.

The Persians did not understand my people. They didn't understand our stubborn insistence on worshipping a God we could not see, following a list of rules and regulations that dictated how we ran every area of our lives. Above all, they couldn't understand our insistence that our God alone was the one true God. For the most part, we were left to ourselves, treated with a mixture of curiosity and acceptance, but once in a while somebody would incite such hatred towards us that we would have to flee to other countries for refuge. Haman was one such person. He hated Jews. He said he hated our belief that we were 'better' than anyone else. He hated our customs and everything about us. The Bible calls him 'Haman son of Hammedatha, the Agagite, the enemy of the Jews' (Esther 3:10). Incidentally, the Agagites were the descendants of Agag, king of the Amalekites, ancient enemies of Israel.

Haman was clever. He needed an 'intelligent' reason to annihilate the Jews, and he used the oldest reason of them all: fear of betrayal. He told King Xerxes of a certain group in his kingdom who had different customs from everyone else, who did not obey the king's laws. If they continued like that, he said, there was nothing preventing them from grouping together and rising up in arms against the king. He had a suggestion: the king should issue a royal edict to destroy these people, and he, Haman, would put 10,000 talents of silver into the royal treasury for the men who actually carried out this important mission.

Like a cunning political strategist, Haman appealed to the king's need to protect himself from perceived threats to his authority and kingdom, and, in the process, offered him the chance to gain a lot of money. He didn't explain how he would get the 10,000 talents, but that was none of Xerxes' concern. He had been told of a threat to his kingdom and he had to act quickly. He sent a royal decree throughout his kingdom, authorizing everyone to take up arms against the Jewish people at a certain date—chosen by Haman—a year ahead. That was ample time for the messengers to deliver his edict to every province in the kingdom as they travelled on horseback and camels. After issuing the edict and signing the proclamation with his own signet ring, Xerxes sat down to drink with Haman—but the city of Susa was thrown into turmoil by the news.

My gilded cage

I was the queen but I lived in separate quarters from the king. I had access to his wealth, and limited power by virtue of my position, yet we lived separate lives. I didn't know about the king's proclamation, and because I still had not revealed my nationality to anyone, on Mordecai's orders, nobody knew that I was Jewish. I led a secluded life in a golden cage, where I heard occasional whispers of events taking place outside but never the true facts. I was a queen but also a young girl.

One day, my maids came to tell me that Mordecai was at the king's gate, wailing and shouting and wearing mourning clothes—but they wouldn't tell me why. I was agitated. Eventually we exchanged messages via one of my eunuchs and Mordecai was able to pass on the news of Xerxes' royal decree. He urged me to use my influence to beg the king to spare our people. I loved Mordecai; I would have done anything for him, but what he was asking me to do was impossible. He was placing the deliverance of a nation on my young shoulders and I chafed under his expectations. And what about me personally? I couldn't appear before the king without being summoned, otherwise I faced swift death. Besides, as the queen, I was protected at the palace. Even if the rest of the Jews were killed, I would be safe, and would ensure that Mordecai was kept safe. I know I sound selfish. My people were facing extinction and I could only think of myself—but put yourself in my jewelled sandals. Just imagine that you are barely out of your teens and win a Miss World contest, where the prize is to be queen over an area that stretches from modern-day North Africa to the Indian Ocean. Your husband is the king, an impulsive man given to odd whims. His word is law and he changes his mind as frequently as he changes lovers, which means anything up to a dozen times a week.

I hadn't been at the palace long. I was still trying to find my way in the whole 'queen business'. It hadn't been easy but, finally, I felt I was getting there. And then, my cousin and most trusted adviser laid on my shoulders the survival of not just one person but a whole nation. Knowing the political intrigue that went on at the palace, he didn't specify how I was supposed to accomplish this task but just hinted vaguely that I was the queen and would somehow know what to do. Of course my first instinct was self-preservation! What did I know about saving people? I was a beauty queen! When I put my objections to Mordecai, his reply was one of the best words of wisdom he'd ever given me. It is also one that has sustained many people over countless years since: 'Do not think that because you are in the king's house you alone of all the Jews will escape. For if you remain silent at this time, relief and deliverance for the Jews will arise from another place, but you and your father's family will perish. And who knows but that you have come to royal position for such a time as this?' (Esther 4:13–14).

Pearls of wisdom

I heard the voice of the Lord in Mordecai's words. He was making it clear that he didn't need me to deliver the Jews. He, God, could use someone else, but as queen I was in a strategic position. Was I willing to be brave and trust him that he would make everything turn out all right? I also heard the certainty in Mordecai's message: 'if you remain silent at this time... you and your father's family will perish'.

I retreated to my apartment and thought long and hard about what I could do. I was little more than a child—a paramour without any real influence over the king, who, by the way, wasn't even aware of his queen's nationality. I fretted. I paced the palace's marble floors and, finally, I made a decision. My cousin was right. I was in the palace for a purpose—God's purpose—and I was going to fulfil it.

I don't want to romanticize my decision. I was terrified because I realized how dangerous my mission was. I know that King David got his ingenuity from the Lord when he had the idea of slaying Goliath with a smooth stone, but I didn't have King David's cockiness and brashness. Even though I knew that David was around the same age as me when he slew the giant, I was still terrified. It was all very well for him: he had done practice runs, killing lions and bears that disturbed his sheep. I, on the other hand, hadn't developed such courage. 'Dear Lord, what will become of me?' I asked. Heaven was silent, presumably because it had already spoken to me through Mordecai: 'Who knows but that you have come to royal position for such a time as this?'

We like to think that because God gives us a vision regarding how to proceed in a particular situation, everything will go smoothly, but it hardly ever does. God promised Canaan to the Israelites, yet they still had to go into battle to claim the land. I might have been put in the palace for a reason, but if I appeared before Xerxes without a summons I would lose my life. My only hope was that he would hold out his golden sceptre towards me, giving me permission to speak. That was the reality.

I am sure that many of you readers have been in a similar situation, when, like me, you understood that God was ultimately in control, yet you still had to face the harsh reality of your challenge. Well-meaning friends and family may have mistaken your concerns for lack of faith in God, making you feel even worse. In situations like that, remember: the Lord understands your fear and wants to walk through it with you. It means leaving all that is comfortable and familiar, but your faith and trust in God will reach new heights. And that was what I did. I dared to jeopardize all that was comfortable and familiar to me and chose to trust God. While I had my faithful cousin Mordecai to advise me, you have the Holy Spirit living in you and helping you in your daily decisions as you seek to live out your faith.

After making up my mind, I sent a message to Mordecai. I told him to gather all the Jews in Susa and instruct them to fast for three days, while I did the same. This is one other thing to remember in times of national or international crisis: we cannot underestimate the value of a united assembly of believers. There truly is power in numbers. Well, if ever there was a national crisis, this was it. The Jewish people faced extermination and we needed to stand together. We sought help the only way we knew how: by calling upon the Lord in our hour of need.

On the first day of the fast, I woke up hoping that, by some miracle, everything I'd heard about Xerxes' edict and Mordecai's words had been a dream, but it wasn't. It was all too real. The dull pounding of my heart assured me of that. On the second day of the fast, I lay prostrate on my embroidered cushions and rugs, and waited in the silence, as Mordecai had instructed. Then it came— the still small voice that never fails to protect, comfort or encourage when all seems lost. I arose many hours later, filled with a sense of destiny and purpose, knowing that the child who had set out to seek God's face earlier in the day was gone for ever. In her place was a woman, completely dead to self but alive to God's leading.

On the third day of the fast, I put on my royal robes and made myself irresistibly beautiful, as Xerxes hadn't seen me in a month. I was fully aware of his sensual nature and intended to use it for my purpose. As I approached his inner court, the trembling in my limbs threatened to overtaken my very being, but I reminded myself of the

Lord's words to me: 'For if you remain silent at this time, relief and deliverance for the Jews will arise from another place, but you and your father's family will perish.' My resolve strengthened, and I slowly made my way towards his throne. The king looked up, saw me approaching—and his smile showed that he was delighted at the unexpected sight of me. He extended his sceptre to me, inviting me to speak: 'What is it, Queen Esther? What is your request? Even up to half the kingdom, it will be given to you' (Esther 5:3).

I gasped in relief and almost fell to my knees when I saw that sceptre extended. I would live! And as for his offer to grant me half of his kingdom, I had to smile indulgently. My husband was as impulsive as ever. I knew him well. He would grant me his kingdom one day and, the next, overwrite the gift with another edict declaring me a traitor, and have me executed without a backward glance. I couldn't expect any less from someone who chose a date for genocide and then sat down with his friend to drink. I told him that I had simply come to invite him and Haman to a special banquet that I had prepared, just for the two of them.

I made sure the banquet included all their favourite foods, as well as a host of dancers, musicians and magicians to provide entertainment. The king was so pleased with all he saw and ate that he asked me again if I had any request. 'Anything, even half of my kingdom!' he repeated. I smiled at him indulgently again. I was still the young queen but now I had finally grown up. I could see my husband for what he was: a spoilt child in a man's body. I told him that I didn't want anything except to invite him and his friend for another banquet the next day. He said 'yes'.

Humans plan and God laughs

My spies told me that Haman had left the banquet feeling very pleased with himself, but his happiness had evaporated when he saw Mordecai at the king's gate. As usual, Mordecai refused to show exaggerated respect and deference to Haman, which enraged

Haman no end. He went home and threw an impromptu party at which he boasted to his guests about his intimate banquet with the king and queen. He boasted about his sons, his wealth and his appointment as the second most important person in the kingdom, and then added, 'But all this gives me no satisfaction as long as I see that Jew Mordecai sitting at the king's gate' (Esther 5:13). His wife and friends fed his all-consuming hatred by telling him to build a special gallows, 75 feet high, and ask the king to have Mordecai hang on it.

At the same time that Haman was scheming to finish off Mordecai, the king was having great difficulty in sleeping. The combination of rich food and dancing girls was proving too much for his digestion. Finally, he summoned his servants to bring the palace records and read them out to him. They had acted as a natural tranquillizer in the past. This time, however, the records woke him up with an amazing discovery: he realized that Mordecai had never been compensated for exposing an assassination attempt against him, just after I was crowned queen.

Just then, there was a disturbance in the outer court of the palace. It was Haman, more than a little the worse for wear. He'd found he simply couldn't wait until the next day. He wanted to speak to the king there and then about dealing with Mordecai. He was ushered into the king's presence, and Xerxes asked him straight out what should be done to honour someone who had delighted the king. Assuming that Xerxes was referring to him, Haman burst out, 'Have them bring a royal robe the king has worn and a horse the king has ridden, one with a royal crest placed on its head. Then let the robe and horse be entrusted to one of the king's most noble princes. Let them robe the man the king delights to honour, and lead him on the horse through the city streets, proclaiming before him, "This is what is done for the man the king delights to honour!"' (Esther 6:8–9).

The king commanded him to go ahead and fetch the robe and horse—but it was for Mordecai the Jew. You can imagine Haman's humiliation the next morning as he robed Mordecai and led him on horseback through the city streets, proclaiming, 'This is what is done for the man the king delights to honour!' If there was one thing I learnt from Haman's humiliation, it was that promotion comes only from the Lord. Haman depended on the king for his survival but Mordecai depended on God, and, what was more, he did not care who knew it. When I heard about his parade, though, my first feeling was of fear. What if, by some chance, it led to Xerxes' discovering my scheme to save my people?

As soon as he could, Haman hurried home, his head hung low. He didn't take much comfort from Zeresh his wife, and the friends who told him that Mordecai's Jewish origins would make him impossible to overcome. They hadn't even finished talking when the eunuchs came to take Haman back to the palace for the second banquet that I had prepared. This time, I pulled no punches. The banquet was bigger and grander than before. I had scoured the kingdom for the best musicians and the most exotic dancers. The magicians were daring, pulling off feats the like of which I had never seen anywhere. I kept a watch on Xerxes throughout, smiling inwardly and a little sadly as he grinned lasciviously at the dancers from Cush. I watched his eyes widen as a magician inserted a stick of fire into his mouth and drew it out again without any apparent damage to himself. Even Haman was impressed. His mood, which had been rather dark when he came to the palace, lightened considerably as the evening progressed. All the while, I prayed for strength and refused to entertain any thought of failure regarding how my people would be saved.

As the banquet drew to an end, Xerxes, sated and more than a little inebriated, turned to me, stroked my cheek and asked me almost tenderly what my request was. 'Anything,' he said, 'even half the kingdom!' I carefully kept my demeanour submissive as I answered, my heart pounding: 'Spare my people—this is my request. For I and my people have been sold for destruction and slaughter and annihilation. If we had merely been sold as male and female slaves, I would have kept quiet, because no such distress would justify disturbing the king' (Esther 7:3–4).

Xerxes affected outrage and demanded to know who had dared to do such a thing. I drew in a deep breath, said a short prayer for mercy and pointed to Haman: 'That's the enemy!' It was as if something took hold of my tongue and put the words in my mouth. When I pointed to Haman, an unknown strength surged through me, the kind that comes upon a person when they realize that they have reached the point of no return. It was an awe-inspiring feeling, frightening and liberating all at the same time. I understood a little of what my cousin Mordecai meant when he'd told me that when he'd made a decision to serve God wholeheartedly, he'd lost his fear of man (meaning Haman).

Haman knew that Mordecai did not fear him. He knew that whatever action he took against Mordecai could only hurt him externally and, strangely enough, would even strengthen his faith. It was Haman's inability to touch that part of Mordecai that had enraged him. I understood all that very clearly now as I pointed to Haman, certain my heart would jump out of my chest and equally certain that I didn't much care if it did.

The rest, as they say, is ancient history. The king was so livid that he stormed out of the room, and Haman fell on me, begging me to save his life. As he was falling on me, Xerxes came back into the room. The sight of Haman pawing his queen enraged him even further and he accused Haman of daring to molest me in his presence. The servants had barely covered Haman's face—a sign of the sentence of death—before one of the eunuchs said that Haman had made a special gallows for Mordecai. Without missing a beat, the king replied, 'Hang him on it!'

Thus ended the life of Haman, enemy of the Jews. Xerxes gave me his estate and installed Mordecai in Haman's position. He also proclaimed a royal edict saying that if the Jews were threatened in any way on the date previously declared, they could protect themselves by any means necessary.

That day dawned bright and early and ended with mixed results. In some provinces, the Jews defended themselves against their enemies. In other provinces, they were left alone, and some people even professed themselves to be Jews because they thought they would be protected by that means. In Susa, where we lived, Haman's ten sons were killed and their bodies hung on the gallows. And me?

Well, I was not content with asking for Haman's sons to be hanged. There had to be more. The thought that my people had come so close to extinction filled me with rage. I wanted retribution and sought to get it. In Susa, some Jews killed 300 men, but didn't lay a hand on their possessions. Elsewhere, 75,000 died, but again there was no plundering. The reports of the killings came thick and fast, and with each report came the sickening realization that I was becoming more and more like my husband. It was not enough that I had been put in the palace and that the Lord had given me a certain degree of influence and power. I was going one step further, using what he had given me to terrorize the people who had wanted to kill us, using the same tactics that they'd employed. I was no better than Haman and Xerxes. Yes, I had grown up, but I didn't much like the woman I was turning into: a despot with a taste for power.

By now, Mordecai was very prominent and revered—if not feared—in the palace and throughout the provinces as he became more and more powerful. The difference between me and Mordecai was that he kept himself in check. He saw his position as nothing more than a tool to further God's purposes regarding the welfare of all the Jews in Xerxes' kingdom. He was not consumed by anger that we had come so close to annihilation, and he was not trying to play God or allowing himself to be consumed with a thirst for power—which was certainly the direction in which I was heading. It wasn't too long before he summoned me into his presence and reminded me that God was judge. I wanted vengeance, but it wasn't mine to give, and my increasing bloodlust was being driven by the fact that I liked having the power of life and death over people. As always, my cousin saw through me.

When he had finished talking, I went back to my apartment and wept for the first time since the first banquet. I wept for the innocent girl that I had been before I came to the palace. I wept because

I wished God had put someone else in the palace instead of me, and finally, I wept because I had become proud and drunk on power. When the tears dried, I went back to Mordecai's apartment and, in front of him, consecrated myself to the Lord. Then Mordecai had a great idea. He suggested an annual festival that would celebrate the day Jews triumphed over their enemies. This festival would be called the festival of Purim because of the lot (or 'pur') that Haman had cast to determine the date for the genocide of the Jews. That is why, to this day, millions of Jews around the world celebrate Purim in memory of the Lord's deliverance.

Everybody needs a Mordecai—a special person who watches over us and directs us to the right path, just as Mordecai did for me. I pray that yours will be revealed to you. And here ends my story, the story of an otherwise unremarkable girl used by the Lord to deliver his people. Today he is still using unremarkable people to fulfil his purposes on earth. When I hear teachings on Queen Esther and how the Lord used her to deliver the Jews, I am honoured, because all those centuries ago I acted not in bravery but in response to the words of a man I trusted, who was also used by God. God speaks the same words to ask of you, 'Who knows but that you have come to *your* position for such a time as this?'

9

Mrs Job: I cursed God
and did not die

I loved my life on earth before the disasters struck us. My husband
Job was a righteous man who feared God and stayed away from evil.
We had seven sons, three daughters, 7000 sheep, 3000 camels, 500
teams of oxen, donkeys and more servants than we had need for. We
were the richest people in the area. I tell you this not to boast but
to show you the extent to which the Lord had blessed us. Life was
very, very good. We encountered no problems or issues that my
husband and I could not tackle together. We gave regularly to the
poor, we were leading figures in our worship centre and we ensured
that our ten children stayed out of any kind of trouble. Our lives
were built on strict moral codes. We feared God, respected our
fellow humans and ensured that we passed on these same values to
our children. Never in my life did I imagine the ordeal that was
waiting to strike us.

My sons and daughters were dining at their oldest brother's
house. Job and I were sitting under the tree, enjoying the cool of the
day, content in the blessing of the Lord. Then the messengers
started coming, one after the other.

'The Sabeans (drunkards and raiders from south-west Arabia)
came and stole the donkeys and oxen and killed all the servants.'

'Lightning came from heaven and burned all 7000 of your sheep
and the shepherds.'

'Three bands of Chaldeans came from the shores of the Gulf,
stole your camels and killed your servants.'

'While your children were in their brother's house, an almighty wind shook the house and it collapsed with all your children in it.'

I collapsed on the ground as a pain unlike any I had ever experienced tore my heart. I didn't care too much about our loss of wealth, but the death of our children consumed me. I lay there and prepared to die. I *wanted* to die. To lose one child is an unimaginable horror for a mother but to lose all of them in the space of a few hours was like a terrible joke. Had the world gone mad? I wailed, rolled about and tore my hair, thinking that it would lessen my anguish. It did not work. I rocked with agony. I wanted to die. Surely it must somehow have been my fault? Surely I could have prevented it in some way? Every mother knew it was bad luck to have all her children gathered in one place together; it was like inviting evil spirits to play havoc with them. As I lay writhing, my husband rose from his seat, tore his robe in half, took a knife and hacked at his hair until he was bald. His face was dignified, even in grief, and his voice remained steady as he said, 'The Lord gave and the Lord has taken away; may the name of the Lord be praised' (Job 1:21).

I didn't feel like blessing God. His name was like bile in my throat. Where was he when the tornado hit the house and killed my children, and what was he doing when the raiders destroyed our livelihood and killed our servants? No, I didn't want to bless God. I wasn't asking for much, just an explanation for the suffering that had become my life. I didn't get any answers…

It took a while but, thanks to my husband's steadying presence, I eventually grew calm. We both tried to draw strength from the Lord God, but how I struggled! Many times I thought I would never laugh or smile again. Even when my mood did lighten for a moment, I would remember my ten children and a fresh wave of sorrow would come over me, and the tears would start to flow once more. During those dark days, I wondered how the world continued with the daily business of living while my husband and I were caught in a vortex of pain.

We went to bed one night and I awoke before dawn because of my husband's groans. He was covered in boils. It was as if his skin was crawling with thousands of insects hidden within the huge pus-filled lesions that were erupting everywhere on his body. I leapt up to help him, convinced that he was possessed by an evil spirit. The person standing before me, naked, moaning in pain and repulsive to the eye, looked like a man possessed, not like my steady, dependable Job. I cried out in horror as my eyes met the eyes staring at me from the swollen red mask that had been a face. They were the eyes of my husband—glazed with suffering, pleading for help, but it was him, not an evil spirit. I cried out again, this time for the servants to come and help me. We covered him in ashes to try to dry out the boils and make him a bit more comfortable, but nothing seemed to help.

As the days went by, the whole community started shunning us. 'They must have angered God in some way for them to lose all their wealth, all their children and even his health,' they said about us. By this time, Job was more or less a fixture on the ash-heap at the back of our house, so that he could douse himself continually. He was a sight to behold, a man reduced to an animal-like state, sitting in the dust, oozing pus from every part of his body and scraping the painful sores with a piece of broken pottery until the blood ran. Nobody wanted to be near us—not the temple priests, not our extended family, not our neighbours. We were outcasts. And still my husband never once opened his mouth to blame God or lament our fate. That was the hardest of all for me to bear. I wanted him to say something, anything that would show me he also had doubts about God's lack of response to our shameful situation, but there was nothing. He never said a word.

Well, I wasn't standing for it any longer. If he wouldn't say or do anything, I certainly would. We had lost all our money, and our children, and then my husband had been struck with a most hideous skin disease. No longer could I follow Job's example and meekly accept whatever happened. What had we ever done to offend God, that he should allow us to suffer so much? We had taken in orphans, given over and above what was required to the poor, offered sacrifices continuously to the Lord, and ensured that we contributed positively to society—not because we were trying to impress anyone but because that was what the Lord demanded of every human being. And this was what we got in return? Well, I'd had enough sorrow and grief. I was going to make myself heard.

I went to Job and poured out everything I was thinking, including my most famous recorded words: 'Curse God and die!' (Job 2:9). Whatever anybody says about me, you can't argue with the fact that I didn't hide my feelings towards the Lord. Of course, Job was livid. He told me that I was talking like a godless woman, and I told him that he was a fool for trying to maintain his integrity and dignity when all else was lost. I didn't know then that my husband was the focus of a heavenly debate between God and the devil. Even if I had known, I doubt that it would have made much difference. What use was a heavenly contest to me when it involved losing everything I had?

If you had everything and suddenly lost it all, more or less overnight, you would understand how I felt. Job and I didn't lose our wealth gradually. We didn't lose our children one by one. We didn't find ourselves trading our possessions over a few months until we found ourselves destitute. We lost all these things in a rapid series of disasters. Where once people had made way for us when we went to the marketplace or the city gate, they now hid from us because our pitiful state was more than they could bear. People used to come from far and wide to speak with my husband because he had a reputation for wisdom and could be trusted to give independent counsel, but not any more. Who wanted to see a man in a loincloth, covered in ashes and oozing pus from all parts of his body? Let's face it, I was his wife and I could barely stand to look at him.

Even worse was the attitude of his friends: they were inflated with their sense of self-righteousness. Everybody had a theory on what was happening to us. One said it was Job's fault that he'd come to this, because he obviously had unresolved sin in his life. Another claimed that God was allowing bad things to happen to Job as a way of purifying him. I guess nothing much has changed since then:

people are still giving the same reasons for other people's suffering. I knew my husband was a good man—the best—and that his friends were all wrong, but the knowledge didn't make me feel better. In their hearts, they truly believed that they were helping us, but just between you and me, readers, it would have been better if they hadn't bothered. At least they got Job talking about his disappointment with God, though—eventually: 'I loathe my very life; therefore I will give free rein to my complaint and speak out in the bitterness of my soul. I will say to God: Do not condemn me, but tell me what charges you have against me. Does it please you to oppress me, to spurn the work of your hands, while you smile on the schemes of the wicked?' (Job 10:1–3).

I think it was easy for Job to say that. He was a man whose life was devoted to honouring and serving God. Losing our possessions, he could bear. Losing our ten children was unbearable but he consoled himself with the thought that it was God's right to give and take—yes, even our children, our most prized possessions. But to be accused by people of having sin in his life, to be told glibly that his faith was being purified by our extreme suffering and, above all, God's silence on our situation—this was far too much. Job wanted to know why it was happening, and I wanted to know exactly what was happening. What was God doing? Couldn't he see our situation? Didn't he care at all? I—we—wanted answers and we wanted them soon. And we got them from the most unexpected place.

Elihu was a young man. All the while that Job's three friends, Bildad, Zophar and Eliphaz, were espousing their particular theologies on why all these things had befallen us, Elihu had been quiet, but soon it all grew too much for him. He had to speak. Dispensing with our culture of deference to elders, he confronted Job's friends thus: 'God is greater than man. Why do you complain to him that he answers none of man's words?' (Job 33:12–13).

'God is greater than man.' I pondered upon those words, and railed bitterly against them before finally choosing to accept them, painful though they were. While I was still processing these thoughts, God himself confronted Job: 'Where were you when I laid the earth's foundations? ... Can you set up God's dominion over the earth?' ... Do you send the lightning bolts on their way? Do they report to you?' and the final crusher, 'Will the one who contends with the Almighty correct him? Let him who accuses God answer him!' (Job 38:4, 33, 35; 40:2).

By this point, I was terrified. It is one thing to ask God for answers, but it is another thing for God to answer out of a maelstrom. Yet Job was not deterred or frightened. Previously I had been screaming for answers to our situation while Job remained quiet, but what I was witnessing now had me cowering and silenced. Job's faith, though, was so resolute that even in the midst of such an awesome display of power in the storm, never mind God's challenging words to us, he was determined to get his answers. So what if God was God and he was the almighty? Job was more interested in why God wasn't answering our questions. In an inexplicable way, I think God was pleased with Job because he did not shy away from his quest. He was a righteous man and he wanted some answers from God and, maelstrom notwithstanding, he was going to get them. Then, when God challenged him to speak, he replied that he knew he was unworthy and he'd already spoken twice without any answers, so he wasn't going to talk any more, to which God replied, 'Would you discredit my justice? Would you condemn me to justify yourself?' (Job 40:8).

As we now know, the fact of the matter is that God's ways are indeed inexplicable. We cannot fathom them or even begin to understand them, as we are human beings, and limited in our understanding. When the Lord explained this simple fact to Job and me, and we actually listened, suddenly our pain became more bearable. We still had unanswered questions, but we had one answer—that God's ways are infinitely higher than our ways. In the end, we never did find out why those evil things befell us, but the Lord restored our fortunes by giving us another ten children and the kind of wealth that can end up being offensive to righteous and unrighteous people alike.

What Job and I went through, many people call the 'mystery of suffering', and having been through it, I still find it a mystery. As human beings, in the midst of our pain and our lack of clear answers, we seek explanations because we think they will help us to make sense of what is happening and perhaps enable us to fix what has gone wrong. When we don't get those explanations, we are like scared children, awake and alone in the middle of the night, looking desperately for someone to bring light into our darkness. I know now, even if I didn't understand it then, that we should not revel in our suffering. No, what we must do is to hold on to God and believe that he will demonstrate his power through our suffering. Not everybody can undergo it, but God knows how strong we are. He knows how far he can take us, and he alone knows the glorious riches he has in store for people who have endured hard times.

In hindsight, I can thank God for that season of our lives, because it gives other people an insight into the difficult situations that they are going through. My husband is the only person recorded in the Bible about whom God boasted unabashedly to the devil. God even gave Satan the go-ahead to attack Job, knowing that his faith in God wouldn't change one iota even if his circumstances did. Many of you have followed in Job's footsteps without realizing it. Like my husband, you have eventually accepted that God is greater than us and greater than our suffering. And, like my husband and I, you have chosen to believe that God cares for us, even if he can seem like our greatest enemy when we are in the midst of our pain. You might not be able to hear the love in the Father's voice when he tells all heaven about your faith in him, but one day you will see him face to face and he will tell you himself how proud he is of you.

10

The end; or Gomer, running woman

So, here we are, not quite at the end. You've heard the voices of women from ancient Israel, and now it is my turn. I am going to do the best I can to enable you to leave this book with a greater sense of who you are as a woman and as a child of God.

If all human beings are cursed with evil, then women are specially 'cursed': with guilt and low self-esteem. I was promiscuous so I was well acquainted with these feelings, only I used them to my advantage: I vented my spleen against men and God by using sex to destroy pretty much everything that came my way. It is easily done.

But before I go on, I should introduce myself. My name is Gomer. I was a prostitute before I married Hosea, a prophet, but I was even worse after we got married, chasing after other men and sleeping with them simply because I could. I thought I was punishing my husband for daring to try to make a good woman of me, but I did not know that I was only destroying myself. You may have been there yourself. Perhaps you have a secret (or maybe not-so-secret) hobby that is destroying you from the inside out, yet you refuse to give it up because you think to yourself, 'It's my life and I can do what I want with it.' Any attempt by others to steer you on to the right path is met with venomous hatred because you think they're trying to mould you into something you're not. And anyway, you like being different from most people. Why don't they get the message? They don't get the message for much the same reasons that my husband did not get the message—and I almost ruined him. Not that he cared too much about that; his concern was for me. His concern was always for me, and that used to make me so angry. Why wouldn't he just leave me alone?

A lot of us are like that. We are so bent on our own way that we cannot see any other avenue open to us. And even if we could, we would refuse to choose that other avenue because it would mean admitting that we were wrong in the choices we'd made.

How it began

As I've already mentioned, I was a prostitute before I got married. I was still prostituting myself after I got married, only people called it by another name: adultery. If that's the case, then I was a serial adulterer. My husband would no sooner find out about one affair than I would start another one with someone else. In fact, after a while, it became a game to me. How long would it be before he caught me again and I could start another one?

The first time Hosea came to the notorious red light district in town (this was before he was my husband), all the prostitutes crowded around him. They wanted to know what he was doing on their turf. Most of the pimps weren't happy either. They didn't want any doomsday prophet scaring their women off the streets. Some of the pimps, though, were pleased to see him, in a strange sort of way. There was nothing they liked better than to bring down what they called 'self-righteous and sanctimonious' people. I can hear them now: 'The day of the Lord is obviously at hand, because you've finally decided to experience sex before you die!'

I thought Hosea would be terrified by the mere fact that he was in such a horrible district, but he wasn't. At least, he didn't seem to be. He wasn't interested in the pimps or the women. Instead he would just walk up and down the road and watch the woman as they plied their trade. After a while, everyone left him alone. He was a prophet, and prophets do strange things, they decided. All that communicating with God was enough to fry anyone's brain. I heard about all this through the grapevine. Although I didn't work the streets like some of the women, I still indulged in the 'oldest profession' when I needed more money to put food on the table, when I'd wasted what I had on fancy clothing and necklaces. Some people said I was just promiscuous. I say I was promiscuous *and* a prostitute.

I never did find out what Hosea was doing when he visited the red light district, and I didn't ask because I'm pretty sure I know what he would have said: 'I was praying and trying to understand why anyone would do that to themselves.' Some of us didn't do it to ourselves, of course. It was forced on us, and we believed that that was the way our lives were meant to be. And if anyone had told us different, we would have snarled back in anger, 'You think you're better than me?'

You can imagine my surprise when the prophet came to ask for my hand in marriage! My father didn't hesitate in saying 'yes'. He wanted me off his hands. He'd had enough, and if a deluded holy man wanted my hand in marriage regardless of my life history, then glory be to God! Father could not arrange the wedding fast enough, so we got married and I gave Hosea a son… and then boredom set in. What was I supposed to do now? It was all right for him, doing his prophet stuff, forever dooming and glooming, but what about me? Come to think of it, what did I have in common with him at all?

Some of you know the feeling. You've been around for a while and you start to have itchy feet. 'There must be more to life than this,' you're thinking. You've tried in your own way to conform to what was expected of you, but you cannot do it any more. You feel as if you're being contained in a box, and if you don't fight your way out of that box, you just know you're going to die. I empathize, because that was exactly how I felt. It was as if I couldn't breathe when I was with Hosea. I needed excitement, not boring repetitions of the Torah. I wanted to wake up in the morning full of anticipation for the day ahead. What I had was Hosea, the doom and gloom prophet, who was also my husband. I needed drastic change in my life and I knew I had to make it happen myself—so I did.

It was so easy that I marvelled at why I hadn't done it earlier. I wanted excitement, so I went out looking for it. Don't 'tut-tut' at me as if you couldn't begin to imagine how I was feeling. I was stuck with a howling baby, and every day ended the same way: hearing my husband's footsteps as he came back after a hard day's lamenting at the temple. He was always emotionally and physically spent. He seemed to think he had the world's problems on his shoulders, which I never did understand. I knew that his job was to bring Israel to 'repentance', whatever that meant, but I think he could have tried harder on the home front. The last thing I wanted after a day of baby-talk was a depressing conversation about God's wrath on Israel and how he yearned to have the people return to him. Hosea's God was invisible and irrelevant to my life. He seemed no more than a specialist in squeezing the fun out of the life of those who served him. I mean, look at Hosea!

We would spend every evening in silence. Hosea was always a morose man and I always failed to cheer him up—when I bothered to try. He was weighed down with his love of the Lord and the Lord's people, and I was weighed down with boredom. It didn't take me long to find an outlet for my energies. I found a man I wanted and went after him with everything I had. Poor bloke didn't have a chance. Of course, by this time, I didn't even care about Hosea: I just wanted to escape. I'd had enough. I got pregnant by this new man, but then he left me, and Hosea brought me back into our marital home, where I gave birth to the man's daughter.

Of course, his holy friends and family thought he was mad. I *knew* he was mad. I was a married woman who had committed adultery in the open, yet my husband didn't seem to care. If he was dying inside from the humiliation, he didn't show it—at least, not to me. I wished he would just banish me, but he didn't. The Lord had told him to love and cherish me, and that was what he would do, he said. I wasn't moved by Hosea's commitment. To me it felt like a noose, strangling me and robbing me of the chance to live the way that I wanted. I was seething with frustration. What was it with this God? Why did he insist on loving people who just wanted to be left alone?

Once again, I was a prisoner in my husband's home, and this time my boredom, resentment and listlessness were stronger. No matter what Hosea did, he couldn't please me. I simply couldn't respond as he wanted. Being his wife meant living under certain conditions and restrictions. I couldn't do the things that I most liked doing, like going to the Philistine temple for a spot of entertainment. Hosea described it as idol worship and sexual degradation. I told him that whatever was done openly at our temple was what happened in people's homes anyway, so why was he being such a prude? He told me to come to the Lord's temple with him to get a sense of the real God. I went with him because, well, what else was I going to do with my time?

At the beginning of this book, Eve talked about how alike women are. Fall bringer or no Fall bringer, she was right. All the issues I had with Hosea were exactly the same issues that so many women still have with their partners today. So many drift from religion to religion, man to man, or location to location, looking for the 'highs' and scuttling off when those highs come down to a stable level. They crave stability, yet take flight at the slightest hint of a settled life. They tell themselves they like living on the edge, but deep down they know that the reason they keep on running is because they're too scared to take hold of the peace and fulfilment offered by stable relationships—and by God. They would rather run away from it, because then they can't mess up. Nothing ventured, nothing messed up.

If that sounds like you, then you're just like me, always running from something or someone. In fact, the moment Hosea brought me back to the house, I was off again, compulsively hunting for my next prey. Hosea still treated me like a queen. He ignored the neighbours' snide comments about his wife and the fact that he was raising another man's child as his own. He simply didn't care. All he knew was that the Lord had told him to marry me and love me unconditionally, no matter the cost. I couldn't believe the man. There were times when I was convinced he was crazy. Why didn't he throw me out? He was certainly within his rights to do so, but he didn't.

The second time I got myself a lover, I actually moved out and started living with him. When I needed extra money to support myself, I traded sex, only this time I wasn't filled with a triumphant roar when I told myself that I was finally living as I wanted and on my own terms. All those things I ran after—seduction, conquest—couldn't erase the fact that the choice I'd made wasn't what I wanted, deep down. To my utter astonishment, I realized that I wanted to go back to Hosea, but I couldn't see how to do it. He probably didn't want me any more. I'd dragged his name through the mud and done everything in my power to humiliate him, because I thought I would punish him for daring to love me. Couldn't he see that I was unlovable? Why did he ever think that I could change? I was who I was, and he should just let me be. For some reason, I ended up blaming Hosea for the way I viewed myself and punished him accordingly. Every time someone made remarks about his promiscuous wife, it actually used to make me happy because they were attacking him where he was most vulnerable. So why did I now want to return?

Coming home

I changed because I suddenly saw the value of what I had abandoned. Those 'dos' and 'don'ts' that used to make me feel as if I was shut in a box suddenly seemed desirable. I looked back at those quiet evenings when Hosea would come home, worn out from his preaching, and gently enquire after my day. In their place, I had cups of wine, artificial smiles and riotous parties that barely masked the pain that so many of the revellers felt inside. The security that I had despised so much in Hosea, I now longed for, passionately.

I see things clearly now. I see so many people who have left the church and then find themselves standing at exactly the same crossroads where I was. They yearn for the peace they experienced when they were faithful believers but they are too fearful of the imagined repercussions to consider going back. And besides, do they really want to give up the emblems of the 'freedom' they've gained since leaving the Lord?

In the end, I had no problem in giving up any emblems of freedom, real or imagined. Living with my lover showed me just how much I loved what I had with Hosea, only I hadn't realized it at the time. I'd been too busy looking at the grass on the other side of the fence, wondering why it was so much more appealing than the boring meadow that was my life. And this time, when Hosea came to fetch me and paid off the man who was keeping me, I didn't hesitate. I followed him. Even when he said he wouldn't have sexual intercourse with me, I was content. I had had enough sex to last me a lifetime anyway. Just being with him was more than enough. I was glad of the opportunity to serve him and be his wife in the way that I should have been all those years before.

We ignored the neighbours as always, and held our heads high when we walked down the street. When the ribald remarks came about his wife, and the comments about his 'bastard children', Hosea would just pull me closer to him and we would walk on. It was harder on the children, hearing people call their mother and father names. They were ostracized by many, and on some occasions they were denied entry to the temple by vindictive priests. But then, slowly, people began to change. We who were once a laughing stock became paragons of God's grace. Where people would once have pointed and laughed, saying, 'Here comes the prophet and the prostitute,' now they pointed and said, 'Here come living examples of triumph over adversity.'

Through Hosea's love, I came to realize that although I thought I was running away from Hosea, I was actually running away from God and all that he offered me: unconditional love, acceptance and forgiveness for every single time I'd done wrong or let him down. Through Hosea, I learnt that I was the one putting pressure on myself, and all the while I was blaming other people for trying to shape me. And through Hosea, I learnt to take responsibility for my actions instead of running away from my problems. Where once I despised the tranquillity and stability of marriage and family life, I now learned to revel in it, because it showed God's love for me and his vision of what it means to be the people of God. Finding stability and security in God's love is not a weakness or a prop to help people get through life, as some have claimed. Turning to God is the result of knowing our true place in life, which is to be in the centre of God's will.

I'm still running, but I'm running into God's arms. I wonder, where are you running?

Women of the Word

Discovering the women of the Bible

EDITED BY JACKIE STEAD

As we read the Bible, it can be easy to overlook many of the women characters. While names such as Ruth and Elizabeth are familiar enough, what of the others, some of whom are not named at all? How much do we know about Abigail, Gomer and Hagar? About the Gentile woman who confronted Jesus, and the poor widow making her offering in the temple? What can we learn from these people and their experiences, to help us in our walk of faith?

This collection of Bible studies, written by a group of women writers, focuses on the lives of a host of female characters from both Old and New Testaments. First published in *Woman Alive* magazine as part of the 'Good Foundations' series, the studies unpack the original stories and show how these women can reach down the centuries and speak into our lives today.

ISBN 1 84101 425 7   UK £5.99
Available from your local Christian bookshop or, in case of difficulty, direct from BRF using the order form on page 127.

To Have and to Hold

Bible stories of love, loss and restoration

ANNE JORDAN HOAD

These imaginative retellings of Bible stories, some familiar, some less well-known, bring to life characters who, like so many of us, struggle in their personal relationships. It is easy to idealize such characters, assuming that they were somehow superior to mere human beings —and in idealizing them, we miss out on the lessons we can learn from their all-too-familiar experiences. Like us, they had to confront complex choices, survive difficult circumstances, wrestle with jealousy, dishonesty and pride. In hearing their stories again, we can identify and share in their fears and hopes, their sorrows and joys.

ISBN 1 84101 036 7   UK £6.99
Available from your local Christian bookshop or, in case of difficulty, direct from BRF using the order form on page 127.

(Extra)Ordinary Women

Reflections for women on Bible-based living

CLARE BLAKE

Have you ever felt that women in the Bible were superstars, some-how extra specially blessed by God? And then looked at yourself…?

This book of down-to-earth Bible reflections is based around the central theme that all women are special in God's eyes. Relating scripture teaching to everyday experience, it shows how God has a special gifting for each of us, how we can turn to him when life doesn't make sense, and how to set about discovering his will for our lives.

Taking a fresh look at the stories of Sarah, Leah, Mary, and other Bible characters, we see how God looks beyond our failures and weaknesses to the women he has created us to be as we learn to follow him, step by step.

To him, each one of us is a 'one off' and in his eyes there are no 'ordinary' women—only 'extraordinary' women.

ISBN 1 84101 235 1   UK £6.99
Available from your local Christian bookshop or, in case of difficulty, direct from BRF using the order form on page 127.

Women of the Gospels

Meeting the women who followed Jesus

MARY ELLEN ASHCROFT

Women of the Gospels retells the gospel stories from the perspective of Jesus' women followers as they gather to comfort each other in the dark hours between Good Friday and Easter morning. It brings to life the experiences of these women, who lived so close to their Lord, but whose voices have not been heard down the centuries. It offers both their individual stories—how each was touched by Jesus—and their common story of discovering the good news that brings light even in darkness. Hearing their voices, at the same time knowing the unimaginable joy of the resurrection in store for them, we too can share in the good news they discovered, giving us hope and purpose in our journey of faith.

Includes questions for individual and group study.

ISBN 1 84101 268 8   UK £6.99
Available from your local Christian bookshop or, in case of difficulty, direct from BRF using the order form on page 127.

Spirited Women

Encountering the first women believers

MARY ELLEN ASHCROFT

Spirited Women is an invitation to travel across time and space in order to encounter lost relatives in the Christian faith. Set during the time of the book of Acts, just after the death of Stephen, the first martyr, it explores the stories of some of the women involved in the early Church—Mary Magdalene, Martha, Mary the mother of Jesus, and Joanna, among others.

Drawing on the author's theological and historical research, biblical study and imagination, this book brings vivid life to women who have been largely forgotten or marginalized over the years. Exploring their experiences and their resilient faith, we too can be challenged and empowered in our walk with God.

Spirited Women also includes questions that can be used for group or individual study, notes for further reading, and a detailed bibliography.

ISBN 1 84101 443 5   UK £6.99
Available from your local Christian bookshop or, in case of difficulty, direct from BRF using the order form on page 127.

Day by Day with God Subscriptions

You may be interested to know that Abidemi Sanusi contributes to *Day by Day with God*, daily Bible reading notes written by women for women. Edited by Catherine Butcher, the notes are published three times a year, in January, May and September. A short printed Bible passage is provided, with comment, application, a suggested daily prayer or meditation, plus further reading to explore.

❑ I would like to take out an annual subscription (please complete your name and address details)

Name ————————————————————————————————

Address ———————————————————————————————

———————————————————————— Postcode ————————————

Please send *Day by Day with God* for one year, beginning with the next available issue.

	UK	Surface	Air Mail
Day by Day with God	❑ £12.75	❑ £14.10	❑ £16.35
2-year subscription	❑ £22.20	N/A	N/A

Please complete the payment details below and send your coupon, with appropriate payment, to BRF, First Floor, Elsfield Hall, 15–17 Elsfield Way, Oxford OX2 8FG

Total enclosed £ _____ (cheques should be made payable to 'BRF')
Payment by: cheque ❑ postal order ❑ Visa ❑ Mastercard ❑ Switch ❑

Card no. ⬚⬚⬚⬚⬚⬚⬚⬚⬚⬚⬚⬚⬚⬚⬚⬚⬚⬚⬚⬚

Card expiry date ⬚⬚⬚⬚   Issue number (Switch) ⬚⬚⬚⬚

Signature ————————————————————————————————
(essential if paying by credit/Switch card)

NB: These notes are also available from Christian bookshops everywhere.

❑ Please do not send me further information about BRF publications

BRF is a Registered Charity

ORDER FORM

Ref	Title	Price	Qty	Total
425 7	*Women of the Word*	£5.99		
036 7	*To Have and to Hold*	£6.99		
235 1	*(Extra)Ordinary Women*	£6.99		
268 8	*Women of the Gospels*	£6.99		
443 5	*Spirited Women*	£6.99		

POSTAGE AND PACKING CHARGES						
order value	UK	Europe	Surface	Air Mail	**Postage and packing:**	
£7.00 & under	£1.25	£3.00	£3.50	£5.50	**Donation:**	
£7.01–£30.00	£2.25	£5.50	£6.50	£10.00	**Total enclosed:**	
Over £30.00	free	prices on request				

Name _____ Account Number _____

Address _____

_____ Postcode _____

Telephone Number _____ Email _____

Payment by: ❏ Cheque ❏ Mastercard ❏ Visa ❏ Postal Order ❏ Switch

Card no. ☐☐☐☐ ☐☐☐☐ ☐☐☐☐ ☐☐☐☐

Expires ☐☐ ☐☐   Issue no. of Switch card ☐☐☐

Signature _____ Date _____

All orders must be accompanied by the appropriate payment.

Please send your completed order form to:
BRF, First Floor, Elsfield Hall, 15–17 Elsfield Way, Oxford OX2 8FG
Tel. 01865 319700 / Fax. 01865 319701 Email: enquiries@brf.org.uk

❏ Please send me further information about BRF publications.

Available from your local Christian bookshop.   **BRF is a Registered Charity**

Resourcing your spiritual journey

through...

- Bible reading notes
- Books for Advent & Lent
- Books for Bible study and prayer
- Books to resource those working with under 11s in school, church and at home

- Quiet days and retreats
- Training for primary teachers and children's leaders
- Godly Play
- Barnabas Live

For more information, visit the **brf** website at **www.brf.org.uk**